THE
POWER OF COACHING

Releasing Surprising Potential in Equestrian Athletes

ISLAY AUTY BA FBHS
and **PENNY POLLARD** MA

Kenilworth Press

We would like to dedicate this book to our loving husbands,
David and Keith, who have provided unconditional moral support and
practical advice. We are particularly grateful to Keith who suggested
that we collaborate on this project, and for helping us create
the framework for the book.

Designed and typeset by Paul Saunders

Artwork by Karen Mortimore

Printed in the Czech Republic

Kenilworth Press
An imprint of Quiller Publishing Ltd
Wykey House, Wykey, Shrewsbury, SY4 1JA
Tel: 01939 261616 Fax: 01939 261606
E-mail: info@quillerbooks.com
Website: www.kenilworthpress.co.uk

CONTENTS

Foreword by CARL HESTER MBE FBHS

Some riders have not been taught how to coach, however, there are now more opportunities to learn and master the skill of coaching. This book is one of those offerings.

There are many important aspects that need consideration in order to be the best coach one can be. This book highlights many of these. The coach's role is to help 'make it happen', recognising where each rider's ceiling is, and therefore all parties need to have different expectations. I've rarely come across someone not trying to do their best, so coaches need to understand and manage the rider's frustrations. The coach can fulfil many roles and ideally should encourage the rider to work on what they can't do rather than what they can do – helping them to be non-defensive and resist showing off. Both praise and criticism are essential, delivered with confidence and conviction. The coach also needs to understand when to push on, and when to leave the problem for another day. Would you, as a coach, deal with a client in the same way as a close friend? Probably not.

In equestrian sport it is more necessary for the rider to have the right support around them to achieve success, including an appropriate type of coach, as talent is not enough. There are cases of riders with less talent, but there are many high achievers who have had the right horses, coaching and all-round support to enable them to succeed, often at a high level. Sadly, some riders with greater talent are not able to access that all-round support and are therefore not so fortunate.

I recommend this book for all coaches who wish to enhance and refine their coaching skills.

CARL HESTER MBE, FBHS
International rider and coach, Team GBR – dressage

ACKNOWLEDGEMENTS

We would like to thank the following people for their help with writing this book:

Keith Humphrey, Jill Day, Nick Burton and Melissa Russell for their constructive reviews and feedback.

Carl Hester MBE, FBHS for his inspiring foreword.

Our friends and colleagues who provided insightful quotes (David Hunt, Judy Harvey FBHS, Amanda Bond, Dickie Waygood MBE, Heather Rabbatts, Heather Killen, Lynn Petersen, Yogi Breisner FBHS, Christopher Bartle FBHS, Phoebe Peters, Amy and Holly Woodhead, Natasha Baker MBE, Jennie Loriston-Clarke MBE, FBHS, Di Lampard, Ruth Edge, Rosie Thomas, Scott Brash MBE, Corinne Bracken, Nick Burton, Lady Madeleine Lloyd Webber, Nick Harding and Professor David Peters).

Tilly Williams (main picture – eventing), Phoebe Peters with Peter Storr (dressage coaching), and Millie Allen (Young Rider European Showjumping Championships Arezzo, Italy), for permission to use their photographs on the front cover.

We would also like to thank:

Core Context Consulting Ltd for their administrative support.

Lynn Petersen, Chief Executive, British Horse Society, and Sara Branch, Cool Equestrian, for their kind offers and suggestions.

Karen Mortimore for her creative images.

Kevin Sparrow, Tanzy Lee and Millie Allen for their kind permission to use their photographs on the cover.

And huge appreciation to Melissa Russell for her tireless hard work and patience with typing and integrating our writing.

NOTE ON HOW THIS BOOK PROCEEDS

This book assumes that the coach has the relevant knowledge relating to a horse's correct way of going for the rider's chosen discipline. The content will therefore concentrate on coaching as a highly valuable competence in its own right, albeit that it might sit alongside other competencies such as judging, stewarding, strategic thinking, programme management, etc.

We will explore the many, multi-faceted issues and opportunities that can affect the clear pathway of development, whether you are a coach or learner. The authors have combined their respective experiences as coaches from the equestrian and commercial worlds to provide practical guidance on how to be an amazing coach. In the chapters that follow we will expand on the concepts and frameworks introduced in this chapter in more depth under the following headings:

CHAPTER 1 – **An Introduction to Coaching** Explaining the aims and key processes of coaching; outlining how to choose a coach.

CHAPTER 2 – **Core** The coach and learner's intrapersonal processes, such as what motivates them; their aspirations; limiting psychological traits.

CHAPTER 3 – **Thinking** Reference points such as the theory of learning; learning channels; barriers to learning.

CHAPTER 4 – **Emotional** Breaking personal blocks; increasing resilience; channelling and managing feelings.

CHAPTER 5 – **Spiritual** In an equestrian context, the relationship between the horse and rider; mindfulness (awareness of self and others); developing empathy.

CHAPTER 6 – **Delivery** Coaching styles and behaviours; delivery cycle.

CHAPTER 7 – **Where Next?** Summary and next steps; the difference between coaching and mentoring; further development opportunities; equestrian forums.

We believe that the concepts and ideas in the book are relevant to *both* coaches and learners, as both parties will need to be open to learning in the pursuit of excellence.

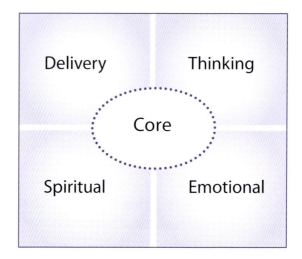

The five areas of competence to ensure excellent coaching.

1. AN INTRODUCTION TO COACHING

POINT OF VIEW

A basic human motivation is mastery: to become more capable, competent, efficient, elegant, confident and therefore more productive in the areas we choose to strive in. Coaching is a powerful assisting process which enables us to develop ourselves and reach our goals, hopes and expectations. Coaching is valuable for all ages, and one is never too old to learn! The need for learning may be triggered by a stretch objective or ambitious target. Life events, for example, a significant change in personal circumstance, create moments of truth that can trigger major insights.

This book is written for the benefit of both coaches and learners and, throughout the text, we make the point that developing and strengthening the coach-learner relationship is crucial to both parties. This being the case, many of the points addressed primarily to coaches are valid to, and valuable for, those learning, and vice versa. Therefore, we have not attempted to make arbitrary divisions of the subject matter into 'material for coaches' and 'material for learners', rather, regardless of who might be viewed as the 'lead' reader at any point, it is our hope and belief that the information provided will be of value to all.

This chapter will explore the benefits of coaching, the role and responsibilities of a coach, and highlight the need for both parties (coach and learner) to be open to learning. This foundation will enable coaches and potential coaches to develop and establish your coaching philosophy (please see Appendix 1 for a summary of the areas that you may wish to include). For the learner, it will address the question of why anyone would want to receive coaching. We are able to solve a proportion of our problems and create new strategies ourselves, but we sometimes have blind spots and/or a clear need for help. Learners can benefit from an external influence, in the form of a coach, who can provide additional and/or different perspectives and suggest courses for action in response to a challenge and/or an opportunity.

> 'Everyone has (at least) one blind spot, and sometimes it takes an outsider to see what we can't. Whether it's your spouse, your boss, or a mentor, that person is your coach. There's a lot that sport can teach us about life and business, and the value of coaching is one area where the sports example is especially strong.'
>
> **HEATHER KILLEN,** CEO H&C TV

EXPLAINING COACHING

EQL Ltd's (the awarding body for equestrian activity) definition of coaching is as follows:

> Coaches help make sport a safe, enjoyable and rewarding experience for participants by taking a participant-centred philosophy. This means that everything a coach does, he/she does with his/her participants in mind. Session plans are designed to maximise learning and enjoyment. Exercises are created to help participants learn. Feedback is given to help them improve. Questions are asked in order to help participants to develop their own problem-solving skills. Everything a coach does should be with the aim to help their participants become independent, self-teaching sports people.

Engaging in learning, whether as the coach or learner, can be exciting and rewarding; and is an excellent way of helping us improve our performance, maximise our potential (of both human and horse), and achieve our goals. Learning is a lifelong quest that can deliver many tangible and intangible rewards for both the coach and learner. Individuals are always changing – influenced by our own evolving needs, such as the need for affection, inclusion and achievement, and by external factors, for example, pressure from others to succeed, or new opportunities arising. So coaching can help learners make informed and significant choices rather than reactive decisions. However, the preconditions for progress, whether for the coach or learner, are a commitment to learning, a desire for mastery, and a belief in true partnerships. One of the goals should be to build an interdependent relationship where there is mutual respect, and trust.

> 'I have spent most of my career without a coach and now try to coach others. In so doing I have learnt how important it is to have this resource in your career, especially as you become a leader in your business/organisation. To have a safe place where you can truly let go and discuss with total honesty the challenges, people issues and personal doubts is invaluable. In the best of coaching both parties continually learn and grow and this ultimately helps to develop those leadership qualities that are often elusive.'
>
> **DAME HEATHER RABBATTS (DBE),** Independent Director of the FA, Chair of FA Inclusion and Advisory Board, Member of UEFA Media Committee

The coach will, of course, learn a great deal from the relationship, but this will be as a consequence of the primary focus being on the learner. The coaching process must be useful and consistent in its application. The learner should see coaching as a major investment towards their success within their area of endeavour. It should not be seen as an extravagant cost; rather it is a powerful necessity in the structured development of the learner.

Historical perspective

Over the previous seventy years the education of riders has changed drastically in a sport that evolved primarily from a military origin to a leisure and competitive recreation. Trainers in sport are called different names. Team sports (football, rugby) tend to have a coach, but so do swimming and athletics which, like equestrian sport, are often predominantly regarded as individual sports. Riders have benefited from 'instructors' or 'teachers' for generations, but modern sport favours 'coach' as the word to describe the educator or trainer who helps the person to learn.

In the business world there has been an extraordinary growth in executive coaching. Twenty years ago, if an employee had a coach, it was usually because there was a serious performance issue. Also, others often viewed the learner as remedial (whether they were or not), so there was sometimes a reluctance to ask for a coach, or engage with coaching if it was offered or 'suggested'. However, the reverse is now true – an ambitious executive would expect to be assigned a coach, often external to the organisation, in

'Having access to top-level coaching can make or break a career; that's true in business as well as in sport. One of the most fundamental leadership skills is the ability to coach and develop talent. Success only comes from realising the maximum potential from those you work with; and there is nothing more rewarding than that.'

AMANDA BOND, Executive Manager, Equestrian Affairs, The Hong Kong Jockey Club

order to maximise their potential. They are likely to start with 'chemistry meetings' to make sure that they are comfortable with the style and experience of the potential coach. They may also have an internal mentor – a more senior, well-networked executive, who can help them navigate the organisation's politics, and facilitate business relationships and opportunities. Coaching, as distinct from formal leadership development programmes, can be more impactful and helpful for the individual as it's based on 'live' opportunities and challenges. The learner therefore benefits from practical actions and outcomes that are relevant to their particular context.

Coaching, in many different environments, is now recognised as an important skill in its own right.

In recent years there has been more discussion and emphasis on the term applied to the role we have in business or sport as educators. Most dictionary definitions make reference to:

- Imparting knowledge.
- The profession of 'giving instruction'.
- To instruct or discipline.
- To prepare.
- To inform.
- To teach.
- To direct.
- Give guidance.
- To order or command.
- To train.
- To prepare for examinations or competition.

On that basis, we think we are secure in calling ourselves coaches and, for ease and consistency, this book will refer to the educator as 'the coach' and the recipient of the education as the 'rider' or 'learner' as appropriate to the context. In some broader contexts, the term 'athlete' is also used.

Core values of the equestrian coach

It is essential that the equestrian coach holds the core values of training the horse as sacrosanct. They should understand that the training of the horse requires clear principles that are consistent in application, so that the horse learns through repetition of those principles of training. It is one of the major challenges of equestrian sport that the coach must not only have high levels of knowledge, skills and competence in training horses, but must also develop the different skills required to manage the training of the rider. These two areas of competence may need different types of development. The coach may be a highly skilled trainer of horses; they may have had outstanding success themselves as a rider/competitor, but their skill in being able to transfer their knowledge and competence to a less able rider may be limited.

'My ambition and passion for this sport was initially focused on riding at the highest level. I am fortunate to have done that, but my challenge as a 'coach' has been to relate and communicate that skill to others. I am lucky to have coached Olympic medallists, yet still help riders at Preliminary level. I get a huge kick from the little tiny improvements from both. Coaching is fulfilment!'

JUDY HARVEY FBHS, international judge, coach and rider; BBC commentator on dressage

CREATING LEARNING OPPORTUNITIES

It seems easy to establish a 'golden goal', find a coach and aim high. Ask a small child who has been inspired by watching a world-class performance and they will tell you they dream of being an Olympic champion. However, that pathway is long and arduous and in this book we aim to unravel some of the complexities that may impede the coach and learner from maximising their potential.

First, there must be an ongoing passion and thirst to engage in learning with an intention of improving performance, that is, learning being a change in behaviour brought about by experience. The opportunity must be seized, even if it manifests itself in obscure ways. For many athletes in various sports, the greatest learning opportunities are achieved by watching. In the modern world of frenetic activity and filling every waking moment, opportunities for taking time to observe are often missed. 'I haven't got time' is a statement often heard from athletes, but 'making time' is essential. In the field of equitation, watching other coaches training horses and riders, working in at competitions, competitive performances (whether live or on video) are all essential parts of the learning experience. Listening to observations and reflections from other competitors can be a fascinating source and insight into the mental state of those who compete before, during or after competition. For some people, listening (auditory) will, in fact, be their preferred learning channel. (Watching, listening and other channels of learning will be discussed more in Chapter 3.) Regardless of the form they take, none of these brief opportunities should be overlooked. A few minutes observation, or one passing comment can impact significantly on learning. Planned sessions, for example sitting in with a dressage judge or observing a coach you respect, can and should be built into the development process for the coach and/or rider. Riders should be encouraged to seize every opening, planned or opportune, to fully engage in learning; to observe, listen, analyse and reflect, so that expertise will evolve from this curiosity.

By nature, human beings strive to be better, strive for more, strive to be faster, stronger and to achieve more than the person going before. That's why we bother to engage in learning. That's why we sometimes put ourselves under immense pressure to improve. The satisfaction is often in the effort as well as in the achievement. As coach and/or learner we should strive to improve, not only the skill we are aiming to better, but the process of reflection and analysis to ensure that we maximise every learning opportunity.

▶ LIFE SCENARIO

A doctor had worked for five decades as a consultant in rheumatic and arthritic diseases. As he moved into his seventies, although he had given up private practice, he still worked two or three days a week as a locum (stepping in when needed). His family encouraged him to retire completely and spend more time on the golf course. His reply was 'When I don't wake up in the morning and want to be a better doctor than I was yesterday, then I shall stop working. While I wake up passionate about wanting to learn more about what I do, I shall continue working.' He worked well into his late seventies.

Whatever reason people have for choosing equestrianism as their sport for either leisure or competitive activities, each individual will have varying amounts of talent. If talent is identified as a natural ability, we as coaches know that riders have varying levels of natural aptitude to ride. Any innate ability will need to be developed through a clear process of training to enable the rider to maximise their desire to improve their skill. Just as a horse must be trained to accept a rider, to develop his natural gaits or his jumping or galloping ability, so a rider will develop knowledge and expertise if they are coached consistently and through good practice. Their natural ability will become fine-honed and educated to maximise their aptitude and ensure a consistent and reliable performance on any occasion.

True accomplishment

Regardless of the specific reason for the coaching and context, it can facilitate general well-being, mental and physical fitness, as well as helping develop skills and technique. In addition to improved performance in specific areas, the intention should also be to help the learner feel more *fulfilled* (personal criteria, such as having a vocation), as well as *successful* (external measurements, such as tangible rewards).

Further to this, a coach who feels fulfilled and successful will have a greater positive influence as a role model for others. This sweet-spot can feel magical, especially when the coach knows that they have made a real difference to the lives of their learners. True accomplishment will feel wonderful to the learner. They will be excited to celebrate their success to date and feel inspired and motivated to continue to triumph in their endeavours.

> 'As a coach you have the ability to change people's lives. Your responsibility is to do that for the better. That role should never be taken lightly.'
>
> **CORINNE BRACKEN,** international coach, showjumping

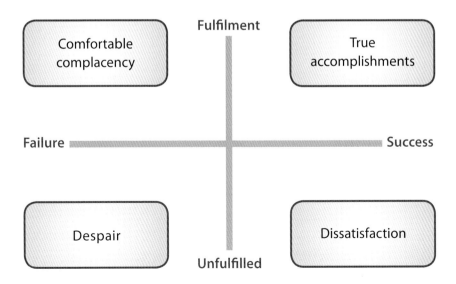

The need for *fulfilment* and *success*.

Avoiding negative consequences

If insufficient attention is paid to fulfilment *and* success, there will be negative consequences for both coach and learner.

Comfortable complacency

A coach may be enjoying their role, but others may see them as set in their ways, and/or providing mediocre results. Their approach may involve working to the lowest common denominator, and will lack enthusiasm.

A rider in this type of situation could be lacking ambition, whereby riding is merely seen as routine or just a fun activity and there is little improvement in their performance and the performance of the horse.

Dissatisfaction

A coach may have passed relevant exams, be recognised by others as a credible resource, and even have won awards, but still be left dissatisfied with their situation if other personal needs are not being met. For example, if they are more of a team player, working primarily with riders on a 1:1 basis may be less fulfilling. If they are socially gregarious, long hours travelling on their own to venues may feel tedious.

A rider's dissatisfaction could come from feeling that the amount of effort they put into competitions is too much, even if they win on a regular basis. Anxiety in this environment could spoil the sense of personal achievement.

Despair

If, over time, a coach is not enjoying their role and is not receiving repeat business, this will lead to a downward, negative spiral, especially if their clients express concerns about their approach and also begin to fail.

A rider may feel trapped in a situation that is neither fun, nor bringing tangible benefits, such as jumping at a higher level. A riding accident could leave an individual feeling very concerned about their overall ability which, combined with some concerns for their personal safety in the future, may take away any sense of potential excitement when they are fit to get back on a horse.

'The Pony Club teaches some vital life lessons at an early age; the importance of managing success and failure with grace and humility is at their very centre.'

LADY MADELEINE LLOYD WEBBER, President, Pony Club

THE COACHING PROCESS

This, without doubt, should be a two-way relationship involving both the coach and the learner. The better the relationship, the more likely it is that the outcome of the education will be positive, developmental and successful. There must be a joint responsibility for the coaching plan and progress, and input from both parties is essential. Success will be dependent on that joint effort and input.

Both points of view will also be important, as this combined information will give the foundation for further training. Although the specific coaching methods should vary according to circumstances, the technical content must be sound, following acceptable training scales. The coaching process and results thereof will ultimately be subject to the ability, commitment, passion, resilience, adaptability and hard work of both the coach and the learner. Firm friendship and a strong partnership can develop where there is mutual trust and respect.

PARTNERSHIP

'To be a respected coach you must have a lot of technical and practical knowledge and an ability to explain different approaches to every eventuality possible. A coach must be able to judge and enthuse their pupil and manage their different ways of learning to achieve their goals. Being positive and thinking well ahead for their improvement is also essential.'

JENNIE LORISTON-CLARKE MBE, FBHS, President of British Dressage and international coach

Typically, the first step in the process will involve the learner identifying their specific needs and researching potential coaches. They can engage in an 'assessment' where the coach can observe them and this will also enable the learner to evaluate whether the chemistry for both parties feels right. Both parties will then need to 'contract' that is, agree roles and responsibilities. A plan can then be discussed and agreed – one-off sessions in any context (sport or business) are unlikely to be a useful return on the investment. The coaching can then begin! Regular reviews will help monitor progress – the coaching process must be successful and consistent in its application.

However, *all* coaching should be situational, and therefore the process and specific sessions should vary according to the learner's needs. The degree of sophistication of what is required by the coach is likely to be higher when working with adults, particularly as adult learners may need help to undo some learning and bad habits, and perhaps overcome their fears, in order to achieve breakthroughs in their performance.

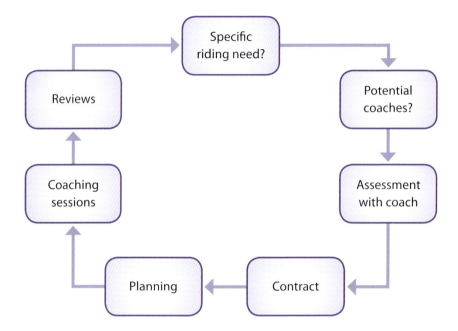

Assessing and contracting with a coach.

'High-performing' and 'high-performance' coaches

Consider a coach who has worked in the riding industry for many years and has progressively improved their competence in a specialist area of the sport, for example training riders with disability, training children, or another specific area of equestrian competence. The coach who develops a skill in that particular sphere of the sport and increases their expertise in that subject area would be regarded as a **'high-performing'** coach with a specialism in one area of the industry.

The coach who has worked in the industry for many years and has moved from a competitive rider status to a coach, as a result of their experience as a rider, will have much to offer the aspiring rider who sees them as a role model. Their technical knowledge of their sport will be high and the ability to demonstrate that technical skill will probably be evident by the list of successes they have had on a variety of horses. This type of coach will be regarded as a '**high-performance**' coach. However, the high-performance coach may have to embrace the need to engage in learning 'how to coach'. To make the successful transition from top rider to top coach needs skills that the rider may not have utilised or learnt to date. If such people have been highly successful, then it is likely that they are positive, dynamic, driven personalities. Often these people are activists (this learning style is explained in Chapter 3) and have dynamically spent their time 'just doing it'. To develop as good coaches, whereby they can deliver their technical competence to a wide range of riders, they must develop the skill of identifying how their riders can most easily take in the delivery of the technical knowledge. While it is recognised that a learner (in any sphere) will have a favoured 'learning style' it is also clear that most people absorb knowledge in a variety of ways and that the 'learning styles' overlap and merge into each other. The following statement may be a reminder to a coach that it is up to them to find the most appropriate way to impart knowledge: 'If the child does not understand the way he is being taught then perhaps it is up to the teacher to find a different way to deliver the information.'

▶ EQUESTRIAN SCENARIO

A top competitive rider of his time – we will call him Fred – who had won countless accolades on the national and international stage in showjumping, was giving a clinic at a venue where many riders had signed up to receive training from this 'household name' rider. A young coach was watching the session (to learn from the Maestro). A rather insecure rider on a rather stiff, uncoordinated horse was attempting to canter a 20m circle prior to riding towards a jump. The rider was incapable of keeping the horse in canter for more than about one-third of the circle. Fred became increasingly frustrated as the poor rider kept losing the canter less than halfway around the circle. Fred repeatedly shouted at her to 'keep the horse in canter'. Time after time the horse fell out of canter and the rider became tense and tired, in her vain efforts to achieve what was, for her, impossible. The horse was too stiff to keep the canter throughout a whole circle and the rider was too weak and ineffective to manage it. There was nowhere to go, because Fred would not allow her to jump until she could canter the circle first. He was totally unaware that this exercise was beyond the ability of either horse or rider. He needed to recognise that the exercise was too difficult and then adjust things to achieve a result, enabling the poor rider to feel that she was not completely useless. The young coach watched with a full awareness of the simplicity of adjusting the exercise for the comfort and achievement of both horse and rider. The young coach at that time had little name or status in the industry and the hapless rider was unaware that the 'Maestro' on this occasion could not help her in the way that the younger coach would have been able to.

In pursuit of excellence

As coaches, we need to position ourselves and our learners between the comfort zone and the discomfort zone; the latter being where performance accelerates, although we should step in before an individual becomes immobilised by the perceived enormity of a challenge.

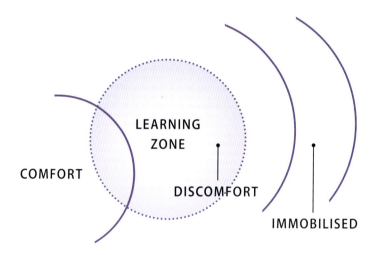

LEARNING ZONE

COMFORT

DISCOMFORT

IMMOBILISED

Creating the learning zone.

The coach should be able to provide both high support *and* high challenge in order to push the learner out of their comfort zone, and into the learning zone. The appropriate mix of support and challenge will help maximise the learner's receptivity, where there is willingness to build on current strengths and take risks in new areas. The learner will therefore feel safe to experiment with new approaches/exercises.

To create this environment, the specific approach would need to vary depending on the personality of the learner. Sophistication is needed from the coach as to when, where, how and to what degree, the support and

ENCOURAGEMENT

challenge are given. The learner should feel a sense of achievement and motivation in this type of relationship: a 'nervous anticipation' before each session of expecting the challenge that the coach will set them and being able to rise to meet it can increase the learner's enthusiasm. The main aim should be to create excellence – however, unintended consequences, as explored below, may result if the coach's approach is not thoughtful, sensitive and well-intentioned.

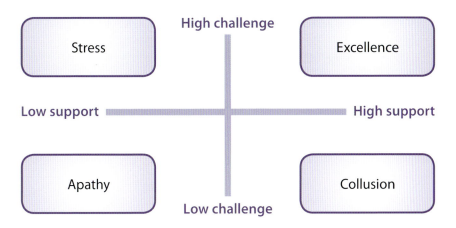

The need for high challenge and high support.

Stress

If there is too much challenge with little or no support, the learner is likely to feel overwhelmed. Their anxiety could then lead to mistakes, accidents and a lack of confidence. But what is stress? You can't see it, hear it, touch it, taste it or smell it. According the five senses then, stress doesn't actually exist. Stress only exists between the ears of the person experiencing it but, to that person at the time, it's very real and, in extreme circumstances, can be seriously debilitating. But stress doesn't have to mean 'distress' or 'suffering from stress'; stress can also be a positive force when it exists to stretch people and challenge their capacity to achieve and thus create greater capacity.

Collusion

If the learner is never challenged in training, then the likelihood of them 'raising their game' in competition or dealing with the anxieties that are likely to be present around competition situations will probably be limited.

Apathy

The negative consequence of a learner receiving low challenge and low support could be: 'What's the point?', especially if there is a lack of interest from both parties.

'The coaching support I have received has proved invaluable, albeit at times hard work! Having the opportunity to talk through my experiences and share them in a safe and confidential environment has allowed me to remain optimistic and develop. I have come through a challenging period and thanks to the support of coaching, I have found the confidence to address these challenges in ways that I wouldn't have previously. Ultimately the coaching has assisted in helping me help myself, to drive an outcome in my career which holds significant opportunity.'

NICK HARDING, Strategy Implementation Director, Canada Life

UNINTERESTED COACH

Responsibility for safety

In terms of coaching riders, we have a responsibility always to ensure that, to the best of our knowledge and judgement, the session is safe and well planned. In these litigious days, when accidents shouldn't happen and there must always be someone to blame if they do, we have a huge responsibility to show a 'pathway of judgement' with every rider in every coaching situation. As a coach we must be able to justify the decision-making process of planning every aspect of a mounted riding lesson.

Risk assessment must be fundamental to every coaching session we are involved in.

▶ EQUESTRIAN SCENARIO 1

In this respect, consider the following circumstances.

Chris is being taught in an indoor school on his own horse in a private jumping lesson. The coach has taught Chris for many years on this horse, and on his previous horse and a pony before that. The family hire the school, which is close to home and it is a familiar place as they also compete there frequently. The school has a good, well-maintained surface and while there is a gallery, people are present infrequently during Chris's lessons and on this occasion only his mother is there. The session is progressing well, Chris is jumping a grid exercise which is well built and positioned on the long side in front of the gallery. He has negotiated the fences several times with no difficulty. Chris canters around the corner, jumps the first fence, the horse stumbles on landing and Chris is pitched forward and falls quite awkwardly on the next fence (only a stride away). It is quickly obvious that Chris has hurt himself and is in a lot of pain. His mother comes into the school swiftly and the coach, already at Chris's side, reassures him and encourages him to breathe calmly and not move. It is necessary to call an ambulance and the outcome is that Chris has broken his femur, is taken to hospital and is laid up for the next eight weeks.

The above was an accident: it was no one's fault. The lesson was being conducted in a well-structured situation with good planning and judgement of the capabilities of the horse and rider and with good prior knowledge of the ability of both. Activities in life carry varying levels of risk. Riding as a sport comes reasonably high on that scale of 'risk sports'. Horses make mistakes: in spite of having four legs to support them, they do miss their footing, lose their balance, trip and sometimes fall. They are carrying a rider (which may be an added 'problem' if they lose balance). This incident with Chris was, in those circumstances, unavoidable; the only way to prevent it happening was not to be carrying out the exercise in the first place. Anyone who rides horses at any level must accept that there is an element of risk that is unavoidable.

▶ EQUESTRIAN SCENARIO 2

Now consider this situation.

Julie is a nervous rider and is riding in a group lesson with three others. She does not like cantering and tells the coach at the beginning of the session that she doesn't want to canter today. The coach listens to her but is also a little dismissive saying. 'You'll be fine'.

The lesson progresses with Julie showing clear anxiety about all the work she is being asked to carry out in the group. Her anticipation of the impending canter work is clear and the pony is becoming more tense owing to the child's anxiety. The coach moves to a canter exercise where the group is in closed order: each rider is asked to trot and then canter to the rear of the ride. When it comes to Julie's turn she again tells the coach she does not want to canter. She is told to 'Keep him in trot then'. Tentatively, Julie goes into trot and the pony, without further ado, picks up canter and dashes towards the rear of the ride with Julie screaming and grabbing at the reins. The pony stops very abruptly when he gets to the back of the group and Julie falls off. She is unhurt but tearful and frightened. She will probably give up riding at this stage!

This was an avoidable accident. All the warning signs were there that the rider was not going to cope with the level of work asked of her.

She was nervous from the outset. This created more tension from the pony, which then caused the situation to deteriorate further. She kept indicating her concerns and actively told the coach she did not want to canter. The coach showed a clear lack of judgement of both the rider's state of confidence and the ability to manage the situation so that the pony did not run away with her. The accident was completely avoidable and, had the rider been injured, it could have been proved that the coach was negligent.

All the equestrian disciplines hold a list or register of coaches. Some will have qualifications and some may have wide competitive experience but no qualifications. Riders should be encouraged to do background checks on a potential coach. It is important (especially with riders under 18) that a coach has attended first aid training and a child awareness course recently and has undergone a Disclosure Barring Service (DBS) check – a search to ensure that there is no history or reason why this person should not safely work with children. UKCC (United Kingdom Coaching Certificate) qualifications are becoming widely recognised as the industry standard for various sports' coaches. BHS (British Horse Society) qualifications are also of longstanding status in the industry and are internationally renowned. Riders should be invited to research the background of the coach, and watch them work. Coaches should always confirm that they have third party liability insurance in place. As a coach, these criteria safeguard you in your professional work. Through any of the equestrian disciplines (British Dressage/British Eventing/British Showjumping) and the British Horse Society the relevant database of coaches/trainers will give a recognised code of conduct, which will help you maintain secure professional standards within your work.

Credibility

Given the demands and responsibilities of the role, and the potential complexity of the situation, a coach will need to develop their personal power and credibility with the learner quickly in order for the partnership to excel. This can be achieved by paying attention to the following attributes.

Authority

Others' perceptions of our authority are likely to be formed quickly. They will be influenced by how we describe what we have done, what we have achieved, who, and what we know. If you are already a recognised coach, then some of your authority will already have been established before you walk into the arena, room, or meeting. Potential clients may also expect a coach to have the relevant coaching qualifications.

Presence

Presence is about attitude and interpersonal style. Our attitude will be influenced by our confidence. How comfortable are you as a coach when dealing with people who may be much older than you, or more aggressive? What gets you noticed? Are you energetic, passionate, clearly present and engaged? How is this communicated through your words, the pace, tone

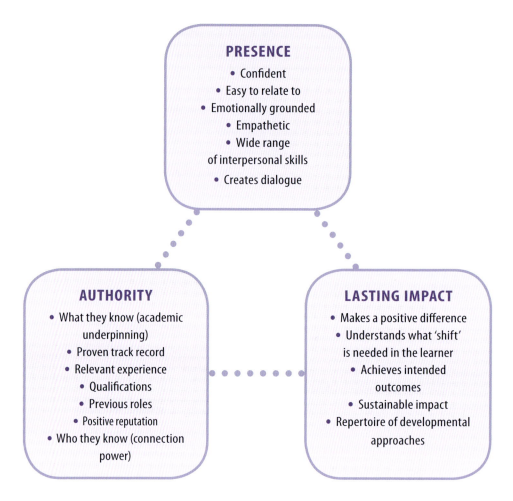

Authority, presence and lasting impact.

and pitch of your voice and body language? Presence is also about our ability (or not) to relate to others, identify common ground and establish a personal connection. An empathetic coach has a wide range of interpersonal skills, and is able to engage in robust dialogue without 'broadcasting'. It is also a skill to show genuine interest in others.

Lasting impact

Lasting impact is the outcome that both parties are looking for from every interaction. Impact resulting from helping the learner identify and think through their opportunities and concerns, and impact from inspiring energy and commitment to take the next steps.

All these three areas are equally important – attributes in one area can also positively influence how the coach is perceived under another heading. For example, if the coach has a positive reputation and has been recommended by another credible coach, the learner may already be 'well disposed' to the person and therefore personally connect with them more easily. In turn, if implicit trust exists, the learner may take more risks therefore breaking through some barriers, which will sustain their learning.

Some or all of the above may be important to a learner when choosing a coach. It is an important skill to understand quickly what will influence the potential learner to make a decision on who they want to work with.

Some elements of the above are reinforced in David Maister, Charles Green and Robert Galford's book *The Trusted Advisor*.

TRUST

Given that trust is an essential element in forming a strong working relationship, they have identified four primary components of trustworthiness, which are, words, actions, emotions and motives. This thinking is presented as a 'Trust Equation' as shown below.

$$T = \frac{C + R + I}{S}$$

T = trustworthiness

C = credibility

R = reliability

I = intimacy

S = self-orientation

Credibility: I can trust what my coach says about …

Reliability: I can trust my coach to deliver what they've promised.

Intimacy: I feel comfortable discussing a wide range of topics including personal concerns.

Self-orientation: I can trust that my coach is on my agenda rather than theirs; and that they care about me.

If the self-orientation of the coach is seen as high, in that they are more interested in themselves rather than the learner, then progress with the other components such as credibility can be cancelled out.

CHOOSING A COACH

In the early stages of a rider's experience they may have learnt from a parent, in a riding school, in the Pony Club or a Riding Club and so inevitably they will have some opinion as to why they are looking for a coach and what sort of coach they seek. Assuming that the rider has been introduced to the sport in a motivational, inspiring and encouraging way, they may now be seeking more specialist individual help to develop their skill.

Understanding a little about how the rider *prefers* to learn is helpful, as a rider will tend to gravitate towards a coach who delivers in the style by which they most prefer to learn. Some riders prefer to have a great deal of information given to them in a constant stream of words (telling style). They want the coach to take all the responsibility for the training (coach-led teaching) and are not keen to take the initiative themselves. Other riders prefer to have some influence on the way the session evolves, and make their own decisions. The rider then chooses activities and exercises and expects the coach to give opinions and help on what they are doing (rider-led training). These different approaches will be discussed more fully in Chapter 6.

A good, experienced coach will recognise learning styles and be able to adapt their delivery to accommodate that style. There is more information in Chapter 3 about how humans learn. Some people like to be put under pressure and driven hard by their coach; others would find that type of delivery difficult and would not thrive under that type of education.

Learners will often find a coach by word of mouth or recommendation. Coaches should welcome observers, recognising that this can be an avenue for attracting new pupils.

All partnerships take time to establish, build, strengthen and deliver. In any coach-learner relationship the parties should ensure that they can speak to each other openly about their aims, aspirations and worries. Being loyal and supportive to each other will bring out the best in the partnership.

In these days of highly developed technology it can be very helpful to have a record of training. This can give the learner the chance to revisit the lesson and observe at their leisure the finer points of the coaching. Observation of one's own coaching can also facilitate a reflection on how a particular exercise worked (or not) and how one might adapt or change it for a different result at another time. Any recording of performance (mobile phone, tablet, camera, etc.), should always be open to both coach and learner. Recordings should be made with the full knowledge and agreement of both parties and treated with the integrity that would be expected in a trusting relationship between coach and learner. Random publication of any data on any form of social media, if that data has been recorded in a private training session, should only be made with the full endorsement of all parties involved.

Commitment to learning

Referring back to 'learning being a change in behaviour brought about by an experience' (see page 15), the experience, whatever it is, should cause us to carry on doing the same, or change something to make the procedure or outcome better. In making a commitment to change, there also needs to be a commitment to learning. If we know what our specific goal is, whether it's a short-term goal (for example, achieving a better score for a specific movement in a dressage test, or jumping a corner fence better across country), or a long-term goal, (for example, aiming to move up a level of competition within six months), our commitment to that goal can then be structured into a plan. This should relate to the time that can be given to the training and the amount of support that will be needed from outside sources.

To truly engage in learning requires huge commitment from each member of the 'team'; there needs to be commitment from 'significant others', such as owners, sponsors, parents, as appropriate, and inevitably there will be some financial commitment. Think of the financial commitment as an investment rather than a stand-alone cost. If a person engages in any type of learning programme, in this case involving a horse, whether the ultimate outcome is a gold medal at a European Championship or a number of years of progressive training of the horse, those involved in that training plan will be different at the end of it. The consequences of any structured development plan between a coach and a learner will always have an outcome, whether it is positive or negative. As long as there is relevant reflection on the process and analysis of the outcome, then the 'learning' from that process can be fully valued and quantified.

MANAGING RELATIONSHIPS

It will be seen from the reference to the need for 'team commitment' above that, in addition to programmes of work and training plans linked to specific development goals, there is potentially a wide range of relationships that need building and maintaining, in order that conflicts are minimised and the rider can flourish. For example, the horse may be shared with another rider; the coach may also compete the horse; the horse could be owned by a sponsor ... in these scenarios they will each have their own needs and aspirations. The coach can play an important and active part in helping the rider navigate the dynamics inherent in these relationships.

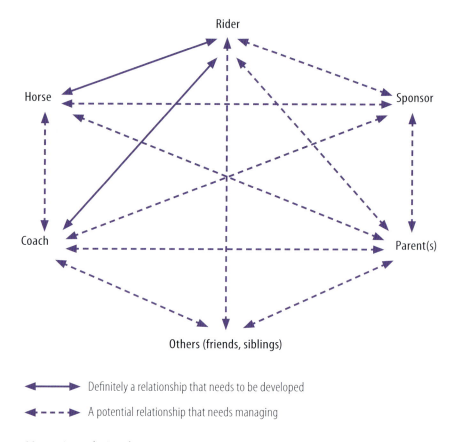

→ Definitely a relationship that needs to be developed

◆ - - ▶ A potential relationship that needs managing

Managing relationships.

As coaches, our greatest hope is that learners enter into an active and vibrant relationship with us to maximise their ability to develop their knowledge, skill and competence through our guidance. For both learner and coach there must be ongoing reflection and readjustment in order to consistently reappraise goals and processes.

As coaches, developing self-awareness enables us to have a clear perception of our own personality, strengths, weaknesses, thoughts, beliefs, emotions and motivation. Being able to identify with the characteristics of the learner will enhance the coach's ability to work with them to develop their strengths and help them to build strategies to overcome their weaknesses.

As a coach you could also fulfil many other roles to your learner, especially an adolescent learner. You may be friend, mentor, assessor, counsellor, facilitator, adviser, supporter, confidante, organiser, planner, fact-finder – in fact you will fulfil a multi-faceted role which requires you to be very adaptable. For example, a rider you are coaching may need help with some or all of the following:

– Buying, selling and/or loaning horses.

– Nutrition.

– Horse welfare and stable management.

– Choosing suitable tack.

– Developing a competition plan.

– Managing relationships with sponsors, and significant others, for example, team members who have an influence on their equestrian goals.

– Identifying additional training opportunities.

– Physical fitness, including that of the horse.

> 'In my experience the coach's role is (in varying degrees) yes that of the educator, but it also forms the support structure, the "listener", "the guider", "the mentor".
>
> **NICK BURTON,** GBR
> World Class Programme dressage coach for eventing, Performance Manager for dressage and eventing for The Hong Kong Jockey Club, FEI/Olympic level judge for eventing, List 1 dressage judge

As a coach you must therefore embrace the modern developments of sport and create a 360-degree approach for and with your learner, for example, sharing and inviting other expertise (physiotherapists, strength and conditioning coaches, nutritionists, etc.) to assist in the learner's programme of development.

Developing and moving on

It is a fact of life that it's rarely the case that a rider will stay with one coach throughout their riding career. The coach and rider should feel secure enough in their relationship that discussions can be had if there is a need to change the training plan. The coach should be mature enough to advise input from another source, perhaps to support themselves initially, or if the rider is moving beyond the coach's expertise at that level. If the rider wants to move to a new trainer, the situation can be managed amicably and with dignity and then both parties will continue to value the contribution that was made during the previous period. The rider should be encouraged to be discerning in their choice of coach. The most expensive or well-known coaches may not necessarily be the best for them. Ideally they will identify a person who has excellent coaching skills, not just a proven track record as a rider, but someone who is interested in making the commitment to help them.

'I have always believed that coaching is coaching whatever sport or walk of life one is in, and would say that I have probably learnt more about coaching from outside the equestrian world rather than inside. To me, coaching is about creating an environment where the subject is confident, comfortable, and willing to learn how to develop and improve.'

YOGI BREISNER FBHS, coach, GBR eventing team

INSIGHTS

- Coaching can help enhance the general quality of a learner's life, as well as improve the learner's performance.

- Excellent coaching requires true maturity and skill.

- The concept of coaching has been accepted for longer in the sporting world than the commercial world.

- Coaching is a skill in its own right.

- Coaching is a rewarding, albeit demanding, role.

- It is essential to understand that people respond to pressure in different ways and that different circumstances cause stress for different people. What you find challenging and exhilarating might be terrifying and distressing to others.

- Robust dialogue that balances challenge and support is essential for individuals to learn and for the working relationship between the coach and learner to develop.

'The moment we arrive in the world, we begin to learn. We did not arrive in the world knowing how to connect with a horse. We had to learn. We needed teachers, instructors, coaches to help us understand horses. And, if we were very lucky, we learnt from people who truly understood how to help us. This book will help us identify those special people ... the gifted ones who make a true difference to horses and riders. An art. A science. A coach.'

LYNN PETERSEN, Chief Executive, British Horse Society

2. CORE

POINT OF VIEW

One of the facts that is guaranteed in life is that things will change. Seasons, weather, day and night. Part of human nature is to strive for both novelty and security in our existence. We feel comfortable with home, safety, friends, relationships, surroundings that are familiar to us. The better we are at recognising and embracing change however, the more we will be adaptable and unaffected by the inevitable changes that life will throw at us. Resistance to change is natural, but as long as that change is 'for the better' we should try to embrace it, thrive on it and be happy for the development and opportunities it gives us. Both the coach and learner need to be receptive to learning, open to change, and motivated to learn.

This chapter will discuss the dynamics involved in transformational change and the need to examine core issues, such as motivation, in order to maximise full potential and impact.

REGENERATION AND DEVELOPMENT

As human beings, we ideally need to constantly regenerate as our environment changes, we decide on different priorities in life, and we identify new goals. In the text that follows, we will explore the stages as indicated in the diagram opposite.

Developmental stages

As coaches, we need to understand that there are different stages of human as well as equine development and that these will produce different needs, concerns and aspirations.

Childhood ➡ Adolescence ➡ Young adult ➡ Adult ➡ Senior

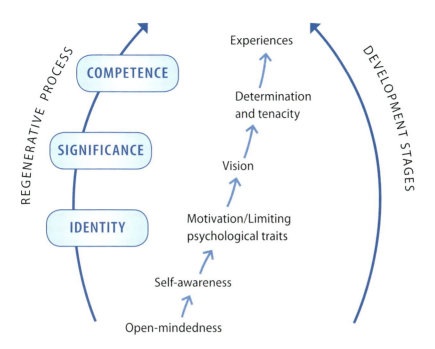

REGENERATIVE PROCESS

COMPETENCE

SIGNIFICANCE

IDENTITY

Experiences

Determination
and tenacity

Vision

Motivation/Limiting
psychological traits

Self-awareness

Open-mindedness

DEVELOPMENT STAGES

Regeneration and development.

Long-term participant development (LTPD) is a model of the athlete's development that was the original concept of Dr Istvan Balyi.

The generic idea has been researched by leading sports scientists and is based around the opinion that there are specific stages in child development. If those stages are recognised and maximised in sport, then the athlete should achieve their full potential without suffering from over-training or over-competing.

TRANSFORMATIONAL CHANGE

Dr.Balyi identified flaws in sport development that included:

- Under-training and over-competing.

- Children being trained as mini adults.

- Training programmes which were not gender-specifically designed.

- Aiming for winning in the short term rather than secure development for the long-term participation of the athlete.

- Failure to recognise key periods of child development.

- Early sport specialisation.

- Insufficient development of core motor skills.

Dr Balyi's concept clearly recognised the following requirements in the athlete's development:

- Specialisation at specific or appropriate ages.

- The quality of practice required to achieve élite performance level.

- Establishing core motor skills at a young age.

- Training relevant to developmental age rather than chronological age.

- Structuring training to the 'windows of ideal development'.

- The pivotal role of coaches in the lives of developing participants.

- Managing the transitional stages of development.

- Providing an appropriate learning environment for participants.

Equestrian sport is regarded as sport that participants may enter in early childhood, but equally may not take up until teen years or sometimes even later. Consider gymnastics, swimming and tennis as examples of early specialisation sports. If a young child is not involved in these sports from early childhood it would be unusual for that child to progress and excel to the highest level of their sport. In equestrian sport, the rider 'learns to ride' and then, at a later stage, perhaps chooses an area of specialisation. Equitation therefore is regarded as a early development, late specialisation sport although this is not always the case.

The British Equestrian Federation (BEF) has established a framework or model to embrace the concepts of long-term participant development (LTPD). This can be itemised as follows:

Active start
The participant is first aware of the sport and what it has to offer.

First contact
Hopefully a positive first experience of the sport, especially with people with disabilities or coming from a non-horsy background.

Active start (boys and girls aged 2–6)
This stage should instil a love of the sport, being physically active and create a 'fun environment'.

Fundamentals (boys aged 6–9, girls aged 6–8)
Maximising the optimal window of trainability to develop basic motor skills. Emphasis on 'fun' but establishing suppleness, flexibility and speed where appropriate, to begin to develop technical and tactical skills. Acquiring the ability to focus, manage emotions, develop a positive attitude through effort and commitment.

Learning to take part (boys aged 9–13, girls aged 8–12)
This phase is important in:

- Further developing technical riding skills to maximise safety and confidence while maximising the window of trainability for motor skills.

- Developing the learner's dynamic balance, coordination, spacial awareness, stamina, flexibility and agility.

- *This phase may also embrace people returning to the sport after a break (often as an adult).*

Training to improve (boys aged 13–15, girls aged 12–14)

- Developing a competent participant.

- Ensuring development of technical, tactical and mental capacities.

- Recognising this as a major phase in relation to fitness and physical development.

- Understanding mental/emotional/cognitive and social development of the athlete.

- *It is necessary to consider and be aware of possible frequent muscular and skeletal changes in this age group.*

Training to perform (young men aged 16–23, young women aged 15–21)

- Developing an adult who is a competent participant.

- Opportunity for all-year structured training.

- Ensuring any other necessary support structures are in place (e.g. nutrition or physiotherapy).

- Annual planning.

- Providing selective competitive experiences to further develop learning.

- Modelling training and competition activities so that structured learning is achieved.

Training for excellence (men 23+, women 21+)

- Confirming and refining technical skills.

- Consolidating all objectives from the previous phase.

- Positive sustainable lifestyle to support the athlete.

- Using all available support to ensure 360-degree management.

- Continuing to improve technique, tactical awareness, stamina, flexibility, aerobic endurance as key criteria of the élite performer.

- Ensuring maximum performance by attention to warming up/cooling down routines.

- Working to an annual plan and considering a four-year cycle.

Active for life: retention

- Maintaining individual health and fitness.

- Developing leadership skills.

- Staying involved with the sport as a coach/volunteer or official.

- Encouraging lifelong participation for the benefit of participant and the sport.

More information on this model is available from the BEF (www.bef. co.uk; *Long Term Participant Development for Equestrian Riders, Drivers and Vaulters*). The model is proposed as an example of an 'ideal model of development' based on scientific research. It is valuable to both coach and rider to consider its strengths and application within equestrian sport. There is inevitably some adaptability within the structure, to maximise an individual participant's ability while considering the underlying criteria. There will also be areas where its specific application is not appropriate for a given situation.

Key criteria for development

Open-mindedness

This is a state of mind. If we are open-minded and forward-thinking, then in every aspect of our lives we learn from our experiences. Whether those experiences are good or bad, if we think about the effect they have on us, then we can benefit from them. The degree to which this state is inherent in us may relate to the way we have been brought up, or derive from the people who have influenced us at various stages of our life. However, open-mindedness can be developed and is an enlightening state of mind to adopt. An open-minded relationship between coach and learner will ensure that new ideas are considered, that there is an unbiased, non-judgemental approach to work and each will be aware that their opinion may not be the only opinion.

Self-awareness and self-reflection

To move forward with maximum effect, whether as a coach or learner, we must develop a strong sense of self-awareness and also an enhanced ability to self-reflect. These should become strong and positive tools for any coach and learner. Throughout the process of developing and achieving competence in a practical skill, the mental skill of 'self-reflection' will lead to self-awareness.

Whether as a coach or learner, self-reflection is one of the most valuable skills you can develop, to assist you in ongoing personal development. Self-reflection gives you the ability to:

'When a coach can teach a rider to develop a strong sense of self and from that become constructively self-aware they have developed a life-long knowledge that is "known" and not taught.'

DAVID HUNT, International coach, President of the International Dressage Trainers Club

- Think about your actions, have an awareness of what you did, when, why and how and to consider retrospectively the effect of those actions.

- Consider your character with regard to the decision-making process in your actions.

- Consider how you might adapt, change, or add to the process if you were going to repeat your actions, do them again, or for a future occasion.

'As a rider the coaching I have received has not only helped me to achieve my goals and dreams, but has meant I also have the feel, knowledge and understanding to be a better coach. You never stop learning as a rider or a coach. Coaches need coaching too.'

ROSIE THOMAS, Event rider and coach

Self-reflection can become a very powerful tool for both coach and learner, but it needs practice and development for it to become a skilful tool in your coaching/learning repertoire.

The great advantage of self-reflection is that it can be practised for half a minute or half an hour, whether in the car (with caution), in the bath, while walking a horse to cool down, or sitting in the lorry after competing. It can be carried out to useful effect, anywhere and in almost any place as long as you use it constructively to help your development. *Badly practised it can become a weapon with which to constantly beat yourself up and punish yourself for not doing better.* A good coach will ensure that self-reflection is only used constructively. Brief moments of self-punishment may be tolerated in some situations (starting before the bell in a showjumping round; leaving the horse's boots on when competing in dressage) as long as a constructive measure is then put in place to prevent the recurrence of the error and you then 'move on'.

Establishing a framework for reflection

In order to explore your full potential, raise self-awareness and make informed choices, we recommend a process of questioning that encourages deep reflection for both the coach and learner, under the headings Identity, Significance and Competence. This framework was developed by Keith Humphrey in 2007, and has been applied within sporting and commercial environments at the individual, team and whole organisational level.

Identity

What are your values and principles? For example, integrity. What relevance do these have in an equestrian context?

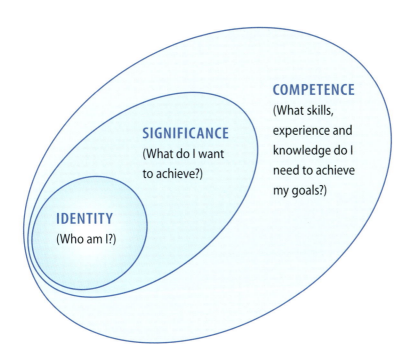

Identity, significance, competence.

What do you stand for and what do you stand against, for example, in respect of horse welfare?

What motivates you when you are riding and or/coaching, particularly when you are under pressure?

Fundamentally, what character traits describe you:
– when you are at your best?
– when you are at your worst?

What are you willing to fight for, or against?

Ideally, how would you like others to describe *who* you are?

To what extent is it obvious to others, what your values are? Are you perceived by others to be authentic, that is, *living* your values?

Significance

What legacy do you want to create for others and yourself, either as a coach or learner?

What do you need to accomplish in order to feel fulfilled?

Ideally, how would others describe your hallmark contribution in three to five years' time?

Imagine you are moving from your role – what is it that you will be most proud of having left behind?

What are your career and personal aspirations?

How much impact do you want to have on others (especially as a coach)?

Competence

What are your strengths?

Where are your gaps?

What are your development needs?

What skills and behaviours describe you:
– when you are at your best?
– when you are at your worst?

What (personal) blocks stop you from maximising your potential?

} In relation to what would help or hinder you in achieving your aspirations as a coach or rider

The following are two examples of how the criteria of identity, significance and competence might be applied to individuals.

▶EQUESTRIAN SCENARIO (COACH)

Identity

Robert is an experienced rider and coach, and also volunteers for several horse charities. He believes in fairness for all, including animals. Robert often takes a stand when it comes to horse welfare, either by intervening himself or informing the relevant authorities.

Significance

Robert has recently started a clinic once a month at a friend's riding school, for disadvantaged children. The riding lessons are subsidised by the proprietor, a local vet and himself. One of his goals is to secure more sponsorship in order to fund more regular training for these students. Robert's personal aspiration is to become the Chief Executive of a national charity in about ten years' time. In the meantime, he's aiming for an official role as a national coach for an equestrian team.

Competence

In order to achieve the above, Robert recognises that he needs to increase his network of potential sponsors and enhance his administrative skills. Robert also needs to increase his knowledge on banned substances for horses and riders. He has started a 'Finance for Non-financial Managers' part-time course in the evenings at his local college. Robert has also applied for the UKCC Level 4 Coaching Programme.

▶EQUESTRIAN SCENARIO (RIDER)

Identity

Karen is a talented rider, and is very active competitively, in her region. Her values include integrity and honesty, which are part of the legacy that her father left her. In all situations he took a stand if he believed anyone was cheating or manipulating the rules to their own benefit. Her colleagues and friends trust her, as she always respects confidentiality. Dressage is Karen's hobby as she works full-time as an HR Assistant for a clothing brand. She recently challenged a colleague, who was not delivering on their commitments; and she feels that the culture of the organisation she works for can be a little 'back-stabbing' at times. At her local Riding Club, during a competition, she overheard another competitor mention to his friend that there was a scoring error on his sheet – the percentage given was too high. The competitor was reluctant to declare the mistake as he had been placed first. Karen alerted the organisers about the situation, even though it made no difference to her own placing, as she was in a different class.

Significance

Karen would like the shows at her Riding Club to run more efficiently, so she has volunteered to help out on those weekends when she's not competing. She is also keen to become a judge, and go as far as she can in this role. Her career aspiration is to get promoted to the HR Manager role in the company she works for – if successful, Karen intends to bring about a culture change. She would like to create a more constructive and positive feedback culture.

Competence

In order to achieve her goals, Karen needs to apply for judge training. She has already started writing for several well-regarded judges, and she has found this very educational. Regarding her career aspiration, she recently attended a three-day conference on 'Managing Change'; and is considering a part-time Masters Degree on Organisation Behaviour.

The value of discussion

It is helpful to ask others for their opinion on how we come across, as we all have blind spots. Discussing and exploring in depth the responses to the questions outlined under the Identity, Significance and Competence headings will help the coach appreciate more fully how they can improve their own performance, and help the learner. The phrase 'to see ourselves as other see us' comes from a poem by Robert Burns. How true! You may see yourself as approachable, friendly, outgoing and communicative, however, depending on whom you speak to, others may see you as scary, bossy, assertive, opinionated and even intimidating. Their opinion is often linked to the context of how they know you. Your best friend will probably know you for all the qualities you see as having yourself. The person who only knows you as 'judge' or teacher will have very different perceptions of you. This must be considered in the coach-learner relationship. Even if you have already identified the legacy that you want to leave as a coach and/or are already on that journey, in Chapter 7, we'll be encouraging you to think bigger, and go beyond your current plan in relation to how significant you want to be in your chosen sporting arena.

Motivation

To understand motivation better, we can start by looking at some scenarios.

▶EQUESTRIAN SCENARIO 1

James is fifteen, he is at boarding school and is a keen event rider. He is in his last year of 'ponies' and has shown good progress with his pony over the last twelve months. He is also a talented rugby player and is doing well academically. Both his parents work, and fitting in training and competition around his school commitments is challenging. James plans to ride at least five times a week and to do this he gets up at 5.30 a.m. and rides before school on two mornings; he catches a train on two evenings to come back from school as his parents are still at work. They run him back to school the same night. One night a week, his parents take the pony over to an arena near the school where James can have a coaching session in dressage or jumping. At weekends competitions are planned around school commitments and additional training on the pony is fitted in. James is already self-disciplined and organised; he never misses a riding session, sets his own alarm in the morning and, while he appreciates the support and assistance his parents give him, he manages the pony himself in terms of tacking up, washing off after work and managing general welfare. When asked by his friends why he puts in so much 'graft' when he could be having more fun with them, James' simple reply is 'I want to ride on a British team some day and to do that I've got to work hard and get better.' James asks many questions within his training; he discusses ideas he has tried when working alone with his coach and is always keen to gain more feedback. He will often text or email his coach with things that he has been trying or points that have arisen as a result of his self-reflection; he never misses an opportunity to watch other riders at competitions and then experiment with things he has seen. He is quick to meet a new challenge and discuss ways to overcome or improve these.

▶ EQUESTRIAN SCENARIO 2

Susan is sixteen; she has been successful on her trained pony, winning many classes as she progressed from Novice dressage to Medium level in the four years that she had him. She competed in some Regional Championships and also a 'Home International'. She loves winning and the adrenalin rush that success gives her is her greatest motivator. She also loves to post her successes on Facebook and gain the admiration and congratulations of her friends. However, the early mornings and work after school are becoming more of a bore, as her friends are all beginning to go off and socialise after school and she has to ride. She has a new younger horse that will need some consistent training over the next few months in order to develop a secure way of going as a foundation for progressing towards Under-21 competitions. Susan finds the training tedious; the horse is good on some days and awful other times. 'Why can't he be the same today as he was yesterday?' she complains. She has pictures of Charlotte Dujardin all around her bedroom and is convinced she will be the next 'Charlotte'. Her coach is finding her increasingly challenging to work with. When things do not run smoothly and Susan must apply herself to find a way through the problem, she is quick to blame the horse, stopping to tell her coach that the horse is being strong or difficult. 'He won't do what I want' is a common statement. At competitions, if the result is not a good one, Susan's mother is quick to commiserate, telling her daughter that the judge didn't like her, or failed to see what a super horse she has. 'Never mind darling, you know you deserved more than that, the judge was just mean' tends to placate Susan briefly. Susan will often sulk and say 'I know I deserved more than that' and her mother will try hard to put a smile back on her face by encouraging her to forget it. Susan is keen to get her coach to set the horse up and compete with him a bit to educate him and make him an easier ride. Her mother agrees that she hasn't really got time to school him but she should just compete him. Susan continues to post on Facebook how hard she is training with the horse and what her competitive aims are. Some of the facts posted are, to say the least, embellished and stretch reality somewhat! Susan will often arrive at a competition and perceive that the judge on the day 'never likes me or gives me good marks, so it's a waste of time being here'.

Looking at these two scenarios, James is what is termed **intrinsically motivated**. His drive is 'built-in'; it is inherent and genuine. He does not need outside influences to fire up his commitment to train and ride in order to improve. He has a clear goal that drives him and keeps him focused. Outside influences can also fuel his already high self-motivation. There may be further support and motivation from those around him and this may be people or events, which add to his motivation. Nonetheless, James has an inner source that continually fires him to organise his life, structure his development and work hard to achieve his aim. Intrinsically motivated learners are an asset and delight for a coach. They seize every chance to draw from the sources around them to develop extra knowledge and experience; they never miss an opportunity to learn from those around them whom they perceive as having anything to offer to their education. James is very competitive and loves to win, but he also recognises that there are no short-cuts and that training is the key to progress. He loves training. He is hungry to take any opportunity that will further his learning and skills. He is innately capable of turning setbacks into opportunities from which to learn. He sees every 'problem' as a way to consider how to avoid that problem from arising again.

Susan is **extrinsically motivated**. Her main drive comes from 'outside'; it is predominantly from an external source. She loves to win and achieve accolades from around her. She loves to share her achievements with those who will support and congratulate her. Her drive is success and admiration.

She will tell you her perceived goal, but the reality of the work involved to reach it is something that neither interests Susan nor fires her up to want to apply herself. If she can achieve the admiration with someone else putting in the hard work she will be relieved. She allows herself to make excuses for herself and her horse's lack of progress, and her mother supports that approach because it keeps Susan happy. Susan allows her mother to indulge her with praise that has not been earned. In training there are always excuses for why something is going wrong or not happening. The coach has difficulty in creating an environment in which Susan actually meets her shortcomings face to face and begins to take some responsibility for them. There is always a reason, and it is always someone else's fault or a circumstance that arose which prevented the successful outcome that was the aim. When 'problems' arise for Susan she laments her bad luck. She can often be heard moaning about how unlucky she is and how things always happen to her. She always has a reason for why she is unable to meet the problem head-on and find a way through it.

In general, the whole family environment is not conducive to supporting the coach in developing a more intrinsically motivated learner. Susan's father wants his wife and daughter to be happy and this can be achieved by placating them and providing funding to increase the quality of horse Susan rides, or changing coach to constantly find support for the mindset that exists in the family. The coach meets resistance from mother when the lack of self-motivation from Susan is mentioned. Father tends to avoid the issues, convincing himself that his wife knows best and as long as he continues to fund the process all will work out for the goal Susan craves. This situation creates a number of issues that will be considered in more depth later this book.

The following examples will show that the motivational factors illustrated apply in many walks of life.

▶ CORPORATE SCENARIO 1

June is twenty-four – she is a personal trainer in a high-profile sports centre. After completing her degree in Sports Science, she went on to study for a Masters in Food Nutrition. June did this part-time over two years whilst also working in full-time employment. She has no financial backing from family members, so works in a bar on Friday nights to help pay the rent on her flat. June is keen to become a guru in her field, and wants to own her own sports and leisure centre in ten years' time. She is passionate about health and well-being and really enjoys helping her clients achieve their fitness goals. June is an excellent role model; and keeps up to date with current research and thought leadership in her chosen field. She engages regularly with more experienced personal trainers in order to learn from the best. June has a client who is an executive coach, whom she has asked to help her generate a life plan, so that she is more likely to achieve her goals. She has offered them some free workouts as a thank-you for their time. After the first meeting, June went away with many ideas, which she actioned before the second meeting. She is fully committed, and enthusiastic about making a real difference to her own, and others' lives. She is therefore, **intrinsically motivated**.

▶ **CORPORATE SCENARIO 2**

John finished his formal education at eighteen, as he found the study commitment needed to pass exams too demanding. He would rather spend his evenings and weekends playing in a county-level football team. The team is on a winning streak, and John enjoys the attention they've received in the local press. Last month, as captain of their team, he was photographed holding the cup they won as league champions. This has also made him popular in his home town with both the boys and the girls! John has started working in the service department of a large garage. He enjoys the interaction with his colleagues, and works hard but watches the clock as he's keen to socialise most evenings. His main motivation is to earn enough money each month to enjoy his social life. He has no particular interest in cars other than his desire to own a sports car as soon as possible. John has not thought about his future – he's happy to go with the flow. John's parents suggested that he meet a friend of theirs who has coaching experience as they are concerned by his lack of ambition and direction and John reluctantly agreed in order to appease them. He engaged in the conversation with the family friend, but couldn't see the problem with only having short-term goals. John was compliant when agreeing to reflect on his aspirations between the first and second discussions, however, and he decided that there might be some benefits in thinking ahead, in order to achieve a higher salary. John is therefore **extrinsically motivated**.

In summary, intrinsically motivated people will leave no stone unturned to work hard to achieve their goals. They are often extremely hard on themselves and may exhibit perfectionist characteristics. They are intense and passionate and often want to work harder than is warranted in one session (and, when dealing with such people in equestrian sport, it is important to remember that, unlike in any other sport, the needs and fitness of the horse must always be of primary importance and consideration in training). Intrinsically motivated athletes thrive on the training and are prepared to explore any method that will help them develop further as athletes. They are open-minded and versatile.

At first observation, extrinsically motivated people may appear to be just as committed, but on further observation, the trait of inherent self-drive will be found lacking or absent. Extrinsically motivated athletes tend to be less resilient to the 'downs' of the sport. They thrive on the successes and wins, but they easily become de-motivated when success is not forthcoming, and quick to lay the blame at someone else's door. They are often more closed in their mindset, convincing themselves and anyone they can around them that they are the 'talented victim' and it is the judge/horse/occasion that let them down. They often state that they are perfectionists in the expectation that this indicates how hard they are working to be excellent, but this is usually a foil for stopping doing what they are doing 'because it's not working' or 'it's not good enough'.

This type of learner is a challenge to any coach. Always seeking adulation and glory, the extrinsically motivated personality will need careful strategy and development, if the coach is going to be successful in turning the learner into a more intrinsically oriented mindset. The first step will usually involve educating the parent or supporter to recognise why the learner is limited in self-motivation and inner drive.

With care, tact and good coaching it is possible to change the mindset of the learner, but this will probably involve some serious soul-searching discussions between learner, coach and possibly other parties (e.g. parents). The learner must first take ownership of the state of mind they are in and the way in which this may be affecting their goal. Then, by small steps of planning and development, the learner must again take ownership of the skills that will enable them to build some self-development through self-drive. Nothing builds motivation like success, but in this case the learner must recognise that the success which gives them their much-desired adrenalin buzz, was achieved through a large commitment – from intrinsic motivation.

LIMITING PSYCHOLOGICAL TRAITS

Perfectionism

Many riders will tell you that they are perfectionists. A rider who thinks they are a perfectionist will often be slow to develop any work independently, and will frequently avoid trying anything that may challenge their apparent competence. They tend to repeat work that they do well, but are reluctant to move beyond that area of demonstrating good work, into areas that may show inadequacy or inconsistency. Most of the riders who state they are perfectionists are in fact showing one or more of the following traits:

- Fear of failure.

- Fear of looking inadequate in front of their peers, friends or coach.

- Fear of committing themselves to dare to make a mistake.

- Fear of showing that they can't do something well enough.

- Fear of 'trying'.

- Fear of moving out of their comfort zone.

One thing is absolutely certain and that is that horses have no perception of perfection. While their rider is circling yet again in their effort to gain what they perceive as 'the perfect' feeling before they make that transition or jump that fence, the horse is inevitably 'getting bored', losing impulsion, tightening, losing rhythm – or any other number of issues might be creeping in while the rider is seeking 'perfection'. If the rider dismounted and took off the tack, the horse, far from going off to practise those 'perfect' transitions, would go and find the nearest grass to eat! The rider must remember the horse as a partner in this working relationship.

Perfectionism is very different from aiming to achieve work that is the best of which you are capable (at the moment). Perfectionism can be hugely destructive, because it is impossible to achieve (especially with a horse) and so the rider will always be disappointed. Disappointment, which is explored more fully in Chapter 4, is another commodity that needs managing in the rider. Suffice to say, if perfection is your goal, whether you are coach or rider, then much of the time you are going to be disappointed and that is not a good state to be in too often.

As a coach, therefore, beware of the rider who states proudly that they are a perfectionist. Explore their definition of the term in relation to themselves. Essentially, a perfectionist is 'one who aims or calls for nothing short of perfection'. The score of 10 in dressage is defined as 'excellent', not as 'perfect'. Encourage your rider to gain knowledge from attempting work, exercises or movements that may not feel 'perfect', or even fluent and easy. Without this opportunity to 'try' then neither horse nor rider can progress. No athlete progresses in any sport without practising to become skilled in the activity. It is how that practice is managed or repeated that will dictate their developing skill. (In relation to horse and rider, this is where the skill and knowledge of the coach in the training of both becomes so pivotal.)

Consider the situation where both coach and learner see themselves as perfectionists. The process of development may be lengthy and slow to progress! One or other party will inevitably be unable to make decisions to attempt work, as they will be inhibited by their constant perception that what they are currently doing is not good enough.

Potentially the most damaging relationship could be the perfectionist coach with an enthusiastic, pragmatist learner, as described in Chapter 3. The coach will inadvertently tend to hold this type of learner back, in their personal quest for 'perfection'. Initially, this may generate increased motivation in the learner as they strive to meet the expectations of the coach they admire and wish to emulate. With time, however, the consistency of the learner never quite reaching the coach's perceived state of excellence, never being quite good enough and constantly falling short, will turn even the most diligent learner into a state of disappointment and then, ultimately, despair.

▶EQUESTRIAN SCENARIO

Amanda is working with Lisa and her pony in a jumping lesson prior to a competition within the next week. The aim is to improve control to the fence and lines of approach. Lisa tends to allow her pony to take control coming towards a fence and then the take-off point can be erratic. Amanda has been coaching Lisa for a number of years and has seen her develop from a happy-go-lucky enthusiastic child rider, who would tend to 'have a go' and then worry about technique afterwards, into a more serious and rather introverted teenager who questions everything as not being good enough. When younger,

Lisa had won a lot of classes on a good 138cm (13.2hh) pony. She has a natural eye for a stride and is positive and brave. The bigger pony she now has is 148cm (14.2hh) and Lisa has another couple of years on him (before her sixteenth birthday, when she will need to move to a horse). The current pony is very talented and, although less experienced than the smaller pony, Amanda thinks that this pony and Lisa have the ability to go far. Amanda is struggling with Lisa's mindset, which is becoming increasingly perfectionist. In the training session Amanda works hard to encourage Lisa to make decisions about the speed and energy of the canter with regard to the approach to a fence. They work on exercises on shortening and lengthening the stride between two poles lying on the ground, encouraging Lisa to count strides or at least be aware of whether the pony has taken more or fewer strides each time she rides the exercise. Amanda sees the pony improving and becoming more responsive, elastic in his ability to adapt his stride and listen to the rider. Lisa, however, becomes less committed to the work, beginning to be inconsistent with her hands, inadvertently disturbing the stride and then, from time to time, stopping and saying 'It's getting worse' or 'He feels ghastly'. When Amanda invites Lisa to identify the regularity of the strides, the pony's response to the lengthening or shortening, or the development of the quality, Lisa avoids making a direct answer to the question and prefers to say 'It doesn't feel as good as I know it can be' or 'It's not as good as yesterday'. Progress is slow and the quality of improvement begins to fade as the pony becomes distracted by the frequent stops and restarts and the lack of consistency in the development of the work. Eventually, when the jumping starts, Lisa abandons the control that was the key to progressing the work and the pony reverts to rushing at the fence. Lisa, almost with relief, challenges Amanda and says 'There, I knew it wasn't working, I've got to get the canter right before I start jumping.'

What we can learn from this scenario:

- The long-term relationship between coach and rider enables the coach to identify developmental changes in the child to adolescent rider, which the rider may not be aware of.

- A rider who, as a child, showed innate talent and had success, moves into adolescence and begins to experience developmental changes that impact on emotions, which she is unaware of and so has no experience of managing.

- The rider is developing perfectionist tendencies which will ultimately be inhibiting her ability to progress.

- With sensitivity and awareness, the coach must recognise that, within the session, the technical work that she has chosen is improving the pony, but it is the emotional state of the rider that is blocking progress.

- Great tact and timing from the coach are required to encourage the rider to identify honestly the value that the exercise is having on the pony. Even if the question is narrowed down to such a degree that the rider has to evaluate the change that is occurring, then the rider will take ownership of that change and can then be encouraged to positively identify its value and progress.

- Great encouragement is also needed to allow the rider to feel good about themselves. Perfectionists are always punishing themselves for not being better.

Narcissism

This trait is not hugely prevalent in equestrian circles. The practical nature of equestrian sport dictates that the coach and rider tend to spend more time involved with the issues relating to the equine partner, rather than having vain or egotistical tendencies of their own. Narcissism may, however, surface when a rider has been indulged extensively in their formative years and developed an inflated opinion of their own self-importance. Usually a rider who spends extensive time concentrating on their own attributes, maintaining a vain attitude to their status and competence, will at some point be brought 'down to earth' by their horse.

Narcissism can be more detrimental if the rider is involved in a team situation, where their egotistical attitude may have a detrimental effect on the other members of the group. The coach has a responsibility to identify any negative traits in riders and manage them appropriately for the benefit of all members of a team. Recognising the narcissistic tendencies of one rider will be halfway towards the coach ensuring that there is no detrimental effect of this rider's behaviour on themselves or on other members of a group.

Bullying

The negative trait of bullying can creep into a situation in a subtle and unobtrusive way. The coach should maintain their own values relating to integrity, honesty, fair play and opportunity for all, with absolute consistency. Leading by example is one of the best ways to ensure that all learners adhere to a 'code of conduct'. This expectation of a certain standard of behaviour may be written down formally (see for example, Appendix 2, the British Equestrian Federation's Code of Conduct for Coaches), or it may be in the form of an 'unwritten' informal arrangement.

Sport is inevitably competitive and with competition come effort, pressure, disappointment, achievement. Coaches and learners manage this pressure and deliver it in different ways. Bullying is classified as pressure that creates emotional, verbal, physical or cyber abuse, that exerts unacceptable pressure on the recipient. It can evolve gradually in a subtle and coercive way or through intimidation, often secretly or privately between the bully and the victim, who shows vulnerability to the pressure. Awareness is the key to managing any underlying signs of bullying. Confidence in the coach-learner relationship will ensure that, if an individual is experiencing pressure from an outside source, they can find relief in being able to share it with someone they trust, in the knowledge that they will gain support and help to resolve the issue.

Quitting

▶EQUESTRIAN SCENARIO

Anthea has been a very successful pony rider, achieving international success on her talented pony. She has thoroughly enjoyed representing her country on a European Pony Team and winning a team medal. The pony has now moved on to a new home and Anthea has a young horse that she is finding quite a challenge. She has moved from a local school to do her A levels at college and finds less time and inclination to ride the rather wayward young horse. Anthea's parents are very supportive, increasing the amount of training she has from her coach and ensuring that she has maximum help at competitions as she starts to compete with the horse. She is enjoying college, has a boyfriend who is not in the least 'horsy' and has learnt to drive, so is increasingly independent. Anthea begins to realise that her priorities have changed and she no longer feels the intense passion that she always did 'to get home from school and ride her pony'. She loves the horse, but is not keen on the training and the increasing picture of hard work and commitment necessary to develop him into the competent, assured performer that was her pony. Her boyfriend and college work are pulling her in the opposite direction from the commitment to the horse. Anthea struggles with the decision that she wants to make, which is to quit riding altogether – at least for a while – and see if she misses it. However, she does not want to let her parents down as they have put so much into the sport on her behalf. She is increasingly frustrated and becoming miserable about the direction of her life, which she feels is no longer in her control. Eventually she shares her concerns with her coach. Her coach has seen it coming and advises Anthea that she must talk to her parents and they will see her point of view if they really care about her. She does not want to be seen as a 'quitter'.

What we can learn from this scenario:

- It is a brave decision to make a choice about a changing situation.

- Anthea feels a commitment to her parents, her coach and to the horse.

- Anthea's priorities have changed and she must decide what she wants in her immediate future.

- Not addressing the issues leaves everyone frustrated and in limbo.

- Discussion and openness with all involved is always the key.

- If agreement is reached, then Anthea is not 'quitting'; she is making a measured decision about her future direction, informing all other relevant parties so that they can also make decisions about the way forward.

The outcome is that:

- Anthea gives up riding for the foreseeable future and enjoys concentrating on her academic work, evolving relationships with boyfriend and others at college.

- Her coach is asked to ride the young horse and the parents continue their involvement with the horse and watch his developing progress as owners.

- Everyone involved feels included and consulted and the best outcome is reached for all concerned.

Quitting may be generated by:

- A loss of interest.

- A change in personal circumstances (financial or otherwise).

- A loss of nerve as a result of a fall or setback which focuses one's vulnerability.

- Any other circumstance that takes away that innate 'passion' that motivates a coach or learner to continue.

There is no shame in 'quitting' of the sorts mentioned, but the careful management of this decision for all involved should minimise the disappointment and effect of the inevitable changes. However, it would be useful to draw a distinction between an appropriate and useful decision to disengage, as opposed to avoidance which may be driven by fear.

Quitting within a training session may be something a coach encounters more frequently, especially with adolescents. The likelihood of the rider abandoning commitment to the task – having a 'mini-tantrum' – arises when the rider comes up against some of the emotions that elicit fear of failure, letting themselves or others down by non-achievement, etc. (see Personal Blocks in Chapter 4). A one-off incident should act as a warning sign to the coach to consider the work plan and progress of this rider. It may be an opportunity to tactfully explore the reason for the 'meltdown'. No training and development of any sport is without setbacks, but any form of quitting must flag up a reason for discussion and review.

POSITIVE PSYCHOLOGICAL TRAITS

Vision

Change is more likely to occur if there are positive and negative drivers, that is, a desire for something to be better, a dissatisfaction with current circumstances *and* a vision which helps us see that the change is possible.

Having a compelling vision of a preferred, more positive future state will provide focus and energy for all parties. A vision is a description of what things will look like and feel like once the goal has been achieved. Articulating the vision of improved performance to others will also help enrol and emotionally engage them in the endeavour. Our imagination can help us 'see' the possibilities; it is a powerful tool when planning developmental paths as well as getting into the 'zone' before an important event.

Determination

It is extremely unlikely that anyone would choose to become a coach of equestrian sport without significant practical 'hands-on' experience and knowledge of the horse, the sport and the industry as a whole. The very nature of this wonderful equine that, for the most part, is reliant on us for his health and well-being means that he demands a huge investment of our time. This investment is intrinsic – deep-rooted, built-in, innate. It is usually accompa-nied by strength of determination and tenacity, which are characteristics often synonymous with the equestrian competitor's personality. If those characteristics are lacking they need to be developed as, without them, the rider will be more vulnerable to the peaks and troughs that are an integral part of working with and competing with the horse.

DETERMINATION

So where does determination come from? If one looks at a very small child as they 'explore' their environment, there is a natural deter-mina-tion and curiosity to 'find out'. This curiosity, if fuelled, can (unsurprisingly) grow. However, if it is discouraged, it could still grow, and then become very dynamic determination. The parameters or difficulties imposed by a number of sources (e.g. resistance from parents, difficulties in accessing opportunity, limited resources) may serve to become strong motivators for the learner. Judy Murray (mother of top tennis player Andy) said, 'Whenever he had a setback it made him stronger.' It is, however, also the case that some personalities react in the opposite way when finding barriers to their progress. Often, the individual's management of the setbacks through appropriate support from parents, friends and pivotally, from their coach, will dictate how they develop their ability to turn setbacks into oppor-tunities for progression.

LEARNING FROM EXPERIENCE

Preconceptions and early 'experience'

Two points that coaches who deal particularly with newcomer/novice riders should bear in mind are that preconceptions can influence a person's mindset almost as powerfully as actual experience, and actual negative early experiences will certainly impact on the way in which a person approaches a new undertaking.

In casual conversation it does not take long to find someone who will offer one or more of the following comments (or similar):

- 'I went riding once with a friend when I was little; the horse trod on me and I've been frightened of them ever since.'

- 'I went riding with my girlfriend while we were on holiday; the horse ran away with me on the beach, I couldn't stop and I've never ridden since.'

- 'Mmm ... horses, they are dangerous things, bite one end, kick the other and uncomfortable in the middle.'

- 'I've always been frightened of horses; they are so big when you get close to them.'

All these observations can be amusing conversation subjects in social situations, unless the person stating the opinion has a genuine desire to overcome the perception. This generates a clear necessity for the coach to know some background information, especially about a new learner. Prior knowledge of some of their negative perceptions about horses can enable the coach to deal sensitively with those opinions and ensure that their guidance and training can overcome these negative attitudes, realigning them into positive and enjoyable experiences.

Learning from the best and worst experiences

It is fundamental to all sport, but especially to equestrian sport, that we 'learn from experience'. It is often assumed that learning is always a positive experience and, as coaches, we should be aiming for that outcome – that is, we should not be deliberately attempting to give learners a 'bad' experience. However, it remains the case that, with appropriate subsequent support, a learner may be able to build positives from an experience that was, at the time, distinctly negative.

▶ EQUESTRIAN SCENARIO

Sam is a showjumper; he has not been riding for very long but is incredibly keen to progress and is aware that a good coach is going to help his aims. He has booked in to a clinic with a top-named showjumping rider. This rider has won many accolades at national and international level and is regarded as one of the best riders currently in the sport. Sam has a kind and generous horse and the horse is looking after Sam at his current stage of experience, however the horse is limited in technique and not too careful, so Sam will often end up with one or two fences down in a class. Sam is training with his top-name coach and approaches a fence (probably too fast and with not much balance or very straight); the fence falls and the coach's comment is, 'That was awful, come and do it again.' Sam comes again in exactly the same way (same canter, same speed, still no straighter), the fence falls again and the coach's comment is, 'Again, come on Sam and get it right this time.' The third attempt generates a very similar result. By this time the horse is getting bored, tired and more careless and Sam is becoming tense and demoralised as he cannot 'get it right'.

What can we learn from this scenario?

The coach is making a simple observation about a weak performance. By allowing Sam to repeat that performance with no adjustment to the way in which the exercise is carried out, it is highly unlikely that there will be improvement. Even if the horse manages to clear the fence, there will be no tangible 'learning' that could be gained from the information that the coach offered. Remember the motto: 'If you always do what you have always done, you will always get what you have always got.'

To make changes in performance there has to be change in application. The above scenario with Sam, identifies a situation wherein the coach is capable of identifying the fault but shows no interest (or even ability) to offer structured advice to improve the performance.

Sam, in awe of the famous, successful rider who was delivering the 'coaching', is very unlikely to ask how to get it right next time. The situation is therefore only going to deteriorate. Imagine the negative and disappointed feelings Sam has on leaving this session. Also, consider the frustration of the coach at the end of an unsuccessful lesson where little or no improvement was shown. More worrying is that there was no visible structure for Sam to take work home to develop and practise until his next training session.

Could Sam learn from this experience? Indeed, he could in the longer term. Once he finds himself a coach who enters a two-way process with Sam of discussion and planning, leading to identifying the weaknesses and putting exercises in place to develop improvement, Sam will recognise the reasons for lack of progress with the first coach. Should Sam develop as a rider and subsequently decide to go into the sport professionally as a rider and then as a coach, he will never 'teach' in the way he himself was 'taught' (with no constructive outcome). He will clearly understand that, to be able to coach effectively requires more skill than just an innate talent as a rider and a strong competition success record.

Virtual versus actual experience

In this world of 'virtual' opportunity where we can view almost any experience through a computer, we can also learn to drive a car, fly an aeroplane and feel weightlessness as if in space, through a simulator. There are some outstanding mechanical horses available that can give a rider their first 'feeling' of riding. In many riding establishments the mechanical horse has become invaluable in teaching the novice rider about how to sit, the coordination of aids to effect walk, trot and canter and an initial awareness of balance and timing. This can relieve a real horse from the effort involved with carrying an uncoordinated, uneducated and often nervous novice rider. The racing world also utilises the mechanical horse in the early stages of training young jockeys to adopt a balanced position, manage bridging the reins, and the adept coordination of the whip.

These 'simulations' do, therefore, have a place in equestrian learning, but learning from genuine experience is essential in equestrian sport because no amount of simulation will begin to educate a rider in the way that horses think and behave. (This topic is covered further in Chapter 5.)

JUDGEMENT AND PLANNING

Judgement

As coaches we have a huge responsibility to ensure that our riders receive positive experiences from their involvement with the horse. As we know, this is not always possible because of the unpredictability of horses but, as with the pathway of judgement that was mentioned in relation to accident risk in Chapter 1, our expertise as coaches is constantly challenged in all our work with the horse. Making judgements about what to do in a session with a horse and rider partnership, what exercises to choose, and the outcome of those choices is the primary role of the coach. There are a myriad of factors that will influence those judgements and there is an ongoing balance between the needs of the horse and the needs of the rider. In every circumstance it is the *partnership* that is being coached. In every coaching situation we are always considering the varying factors and then making active decisions as we work in, about whether the help or correction is directed at the rider (e.g. position, use and effect of aids) or at the way of going of the horse (e.g. more rhythm, energy.) The following are just a few of the factors to be borne in mind:

- Age of horse.

- Age of rider.

- Fitness of horse.

- Fitness of rider.

- Level to which the horse has been trained.

- Reason for the session (imminent competition or ongoing training).

- Time available (e.g. 10 minutes before a test or showjumping round, or full allocated training session of 40 minutes).

- Facilities available (e.g. indoor/outdoor school, field, beach, hacking down the lane).

- Competence of coach.

- Commitment and mental state of rider.

- Mental state of horse.

- Past history (horse or rider).

- Confidence of horse/rider.

Planning

As a coach it is important to plan a session so that learning from that session is maximised.

The more experience the coach has, the more that ability to 'plan' a session becomes automatic and fairly instant. However, one of the short-comings of many experienced coaches is that this process of 'planning' a session becomes so automatic through years of experience that the plan is never discussed with the rider. The rider is then trained through the session which is entirely led and regulated by the coach – 'a coach-led session'. In many instances the coach will defend this action by saying 'That's why the rider comes, to benefit from my expertise.' This is true, but if the coach makes all the decisions in relation to:

- What to work on ...

- What exercises to use for improvement ...

- When to work in trot or canter ...

- When to change the rein or give the horse a rest, and

- When to conclude the work and cool down ...

then the rider takes no part in the lesson other than carrying out the instructions of the coach. The rider is not involved in decision-making, and may not even be asked for any input on what is happening. The coach maintains *total* control of the proceedings, based on what they are observing from the ground as the session progresses.

The rider can only effectively gain benefit from this experience, if there is some two-way communication between coach and rider.

To be effective, the coach must observe every partnership with 'fresh eyes'. However well they know the partnership, watching the initial work is hugely beneficial in the decision-making process for the imminent training session. Therefore, no assumptions should be made, such as: 'I know the horse so well, he always starts a bit tense'; 'I know the rider is always slow to get going and likes to walk for ten minutes before she starts.'

It is even worse if the coach is also a judge and makes assumptions, such as: 'I never give this horse more than 6 for his walk, it's never worth more.' The rider could have been on a two-week training course with a wonderful coach who has concentrated on developing the walk and this coach is prejudging before the horse has even come down the centre line! This highlights the dangers of assumptions based on past knowledge and, if habitual, can lead to poor coaching and poor judging!

As a coach you will develop a far stronger relationship with your rider if you involve them in the decision-making from the earliest opportunity. By sharing your knowledge (which is, of course, greater and has more depth than theirs – which is why they are having lessons with you), you broaden your opportunity to use that knowledge to maximise your rider's experience. By involving them, not only will you have more understanding of their knowledge of a subject, but you will hand some of the responsibility to them and they then share the responsibility for the learning process.

If/when things go wrong or not according to a shared plan, there can be a joint responsibility for the issues which can then be discussed, to agree an outcome of management.

▶EQUESTRIAN SCENARIO 1

Fred is lungeing his horse for exercise and also to learn how to improve the horse's gaits by working him from the ground. The rein contact is poor, the horse is unruly and badly behaved and both Fred and the horse are clearly not benefiting from the experience. A coach offers to give some assistance and first asks Fred to stop and have a chat. The coach asks the following questions:

Q 'Why do you hold the rein like that?'
A 'That's the way I was told to hold it.'

Q 'Why do you twist the lash of the whip up every time you try to change the rein?'
A 'That's what I was told I had to do.'

Q 'Would it help if you moved a little to encourage the horse to stay more actively in front of you?'
A 'I was told I had to stand still when lungeing.'

The coach's following question to all Fred's answers was 'WHY?'

Fred could give no reason for any of the instructions that he had been 'told he must carry out'. If those instructions then prove either difficult to carry out or do not have an outcome that is progressive towards improvement, there must be some argument for changing the procedure or asking 'Why do it that way?'

Fred is operating in a very limiting environment, where there has been no discussion about why he should do things in a particular way (e.g. safety, ease of handling, good practice, etc.). He has not shown any initiative to ask 'Why?' He may in fact feel unable to ask this question (for fear of appearing an idiot, being told off for not knowing, belittlement for daring to ask, etc.). The situation in which he finds himself is likely to demoralise him. He will not achieve improvement from the horse and so the motivation from a positive outcome will not be forthcoming.

▶ EQUESTRIAN SCENARIO 2

Sue is also learning to lunge a horse. Her coach works with her initially, showing her two or three safe and easy ways to hold the rein. The coach explains that Sue may favour one way and become familiar with that if it works for her, but there may be occasions (e.g. if a horse is very strong) when she may experiment with a different system (e.g. rein in two hands rather than one) and that such variation can be useful and further develop her skill. Sue is encouraged to manage the long and unwieldy lunge whip, being shown a couple of techniques for dealing with the long lash. The coach discusses the principle that, ideally, the more still one can stand the more likely it is that the horse will work to a contact on a true circle, but also explains that this is easy with a trained horse but often, with a lazy or uneducated horse, it may be necessary to move a little and stay in a position of 'keeping the horse slightly in front of you to keep him active'. The coach gives Sue the opportunity to practise lungeing and discusses with her what she felt about the work afterwards.

Fred has been told *what* to do but not *why* or *how* to do it. When he finds things difficult he feels detached from his coach and not able to identify his concerns. His isolation is increased by his sense of his own failure or inability to learn how to lunge the horse satisfactorily.

Sue has been well supported by her coach throughout the process, with clear information given, with options for *how* and reasons for *why*. In this situation Sue feels well advised and, when starting to practise, feels able to discuss how she is getting on with her coach. Even if Sue finds it difficult she is unlikely to feel the isolation and inadequacy that Fred feels because her coach is there to support her step by step.

INSIGHTS

- The learner's full potential will only be maximised if attention is paid to their psychological process and general well-being, as well as developing their technical ability.

- A learner who is intrinsically motivated will be easier to work with than someone who is extrinsically motivated.

- For the coach and learner to maximise their potential, they must be open to change and be prepared to regenerate constantly.

- Open-mindedness is the initial key which facilitates access to amazing opportunities.

- Self-reflection should be mastered as an essential skill in the learning process.

- Coaches must have the patience to explore and listen to the specific requirements of the learner that are particular to their stage of development, and avoid making assumptions based on stereotypes.

3. THINKING

POINT OF VIEW

A great coach needs an in-depth knowledge of learning and human nature, in order to create a strong foundation for practical application.

This chapter will highlight models relating to learning channels and styles, mindsets, critical analysis, barriers to learning and role models.

CONCEPTS RELATING TO LEARNING

When giving a clinic or workshop, we are often asked the question: 'What is learning?' Usually the answers range from: 'Gaining knowledge', 'Developing a new skill' to 'Being informed' and 'Taking in new information.' All these definitions would be found in most dictionaries.

When, within the discussion, we introduce the thought that all these definitions tend to imply a positive experience in learning, immediately a bad experience will be volunteered. Especially where horses are concerned, we have often heard 'I had a riding lesson once and the horse ran away with me, so I've never ridden since!' In most cases, when asked to describe a learning event, most people will be as vivid in their recollection of a bad experience as they will of a good experience.

It is the responsibility of the coach to deliver 'teaching or education' in such a way that, for the most part a 'positive learning experience' is the outcome. This, in turn, will lead to motivation and increased desire for more input. In the same discussion it is easy to find the 'bad experience' and, while this can be a de-motivator or turn-off, if managed well by both coach and learner, it can turn into a positive learning experience whereby the mistake becomes the tool for correction, improvement and transformation.

LEARNING 'HOW TO LEARN'

The appetite for learning can often vary depending on an individual's age. Children are often more adventurous and curious than adults, less embarrassed when trying things out, and less aware of the potential risks of a particular course of action. However, at any age, the learner needs to learn how to learn (and in some cases unlearn unproductive habits), in order to move forward. We can get stuck in patterns of behaviour even if we want a different outcome. The learner may need to reframe their view, that is, reframing a problem into an opportunity. In some cultures the attitude is: 'Everything's a useful experience, unless you die'!

> 'From my riding career point of view, which I presume also followed into the coaching, came the expression: "Pride must not stop progress".'
>
> **YOGI BREISNER FBHS,** coach, GBR Eventing Team

The learning cycle

So, we learn from an experience which may be good or bad. As a result of that experience we consider, review and reflect on the experience. From this reflection we draw conclusions. The conclusions then guide us to change the experience, or, if it was a good one, to repeat it to the best of our ability. The ongoing cycle of learning should be the foundation of all the coach and learner do.

> 'I learnt more from sitting on the sidelines (owing to injury) and observing . . . watching others make mistakes and learning from them.'
>
> **HOLLY WOODHEAD,** rider, GBR Eventing Team

The educationalist David Kolb was the first to establish a recognised 'cycle of learning', as represented in the diagram overleaf. This ongoing cycle, involving experiences and reflection on those experiences, helps develop secure values in what both coach and learner practise. Experience becomes the wisdom gained by the changes and trials of life in general but, in our context, specifically in equestrian activity. These assist the coach and learner

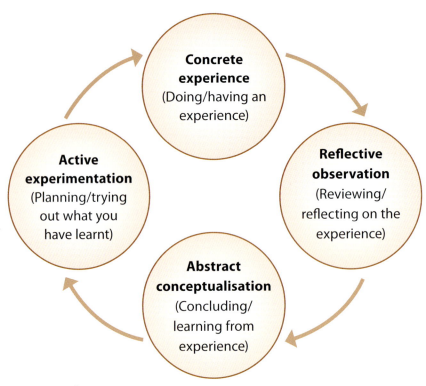

Learning cycle.

to evolve through the weakness and flexibility of a sapling – blown this way and that depending on the direction of the prevailing wind (influence) – into the strong, secure, deeply-rooted confidence brought by maturity, and secure knowledge drawn from experience.

STRONG FOUNDATIONS

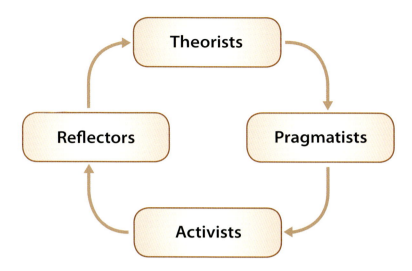

Honey and Mumford's learning styles.

Types of thinking and learning

Honey and Mumford evolved Kolb's model into the four main types of thinking illustrated in the diagram above.

The characteristics of these can be summarised as follows:

The theorist:

- Is a contemplative learner.

- Is often a perfectionist, more detached and objective than others.

- Likes to be sure of the 'theory' behind something. Likes information and to be able to work things out by applying the model or theory.

The pragmatist:

- Will solve problems.

- Needs to know the relevance of what they are doing and whether it works.

- Likes to try things out.

- Likes to 'have a go' and not spend too much time theorising.

The activist:

- Wants to get on and try a new experience by doing it.

- Learns by trial and error.

- Is creative and thrives on a challenge.

- Is quick to take part, doesn't mind being put on the spot.

- Thinks out loud and is impatient if 'talked at' for too long.

The reflector:

- Is a thinking learner.

- Likes time to think things through first.

- Likes to watch others try first.

- Appears tolerant and patient.

- Will often listen to the opinions of others before speaking or doing.

By way of example, ask yourself the question: if you bought a new car, would you read the manual from front to back in order to understand the car (theorist approach); or would you learn about the car's features by pressing different buttons and seeing what happens (activist)? Would you prefer to understand the background, context and relevance of an exercise or activity before fully engaging (pragmatist); or do you like to spend quiet time on your own to make sense of situations and draw your own conclusions (reflector)?

We all use all of these methods but they are like muscles – some are more well-developed and therefore more valued than others.

In order to maximise our learning we may need to engage in all areas and methods, but particularly more fully in our *least* preferred learning style. For example, the person who prefers to *reflect*, may need to be more of an *activist*.

Whether coach or learner, it will be helpful to identify a personal preference for how you as an individual learn best. The following questions may provide some clues:

Do you need to see something happening *before* you really grasp the concept of a piece of work or exercise?

Do you need to have a *full* explanation from others before you even contemplate trying something new?

Do you need to *'have a go'* and try to feel and experience the exercise practically, to be able to begin to grasp it?

Do you need opportunities to stand back and consider situations before you jump in?

In summary:

- If you like to seize something new and 'have a go', you are an *activist* learner.

- If you are fairly practical and will give it a go while finding out as you progress what works and what doesn't, you are a *pragmatist* learner.

- If you like to observe someone else carrying out the task and then think about it, perhaps asking some questions to clarify, before attempting it yourself, you are a *reflector* learner.

- If you like to know all the theory behind a concept before you think of trying it, you are a *theorist* learner.

Depending on circumstances, we absorb new information or experiences in different ways. It is pivotal for the coach to recognise the variety of ways in which the learner may (or may not) be receptive to coaching and be able to adapt, sometimes quite quickly, to maximise the learning experience.

'My turning point with my riding was when I was thirteen and Mum said "You have to learn to ride what you've got." She said: "Amy you must go into the arena and make the best you can on that horse." It's not about winning; it's about learning.'

AMY WOODHEAD, second rider to Carl Hester MBE, FBHS; represented GBR as a young rider

Cycle of action learning

Learning will be more meaningful when all of the above stages are followed with specific actions. This process is sometimes referred to as the 'cycle of action learning' (Revans, 1982), as shown in the diagram overleaf.

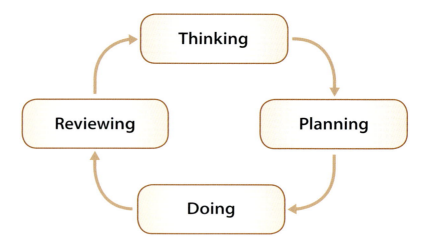

Action learning cycle.

Single loop and double loop learning

Professor Chris Argyris of Harvard has become well known for his distinction between 'single loop' and 'double loop' learning. The former is about the correction of errors; the latter is about questioning fundamental views. Double loop learning involves re-examination of the fundamentals, which may lead to *unlearning* previously held views.

Learning channels

So, the coach's role is to impart learning to the learners. If only it were so easy! Let's consider some of the methods of transferring that knowledge and some of the barriers that can limit learning. We naturally absorb information through the channels of seeing (visual), hearing (auditory) and doing (kinaesthetically).

Learning channels.

We all have personal preferences as to how we both give and receive information. However, learning opportunities will be maximised if *all* the above channels are used. The language that a rider uses will provide clues as to their preferred channel, for example: 'I become tense when I'm surrounded by loud, continuous noise' (auditory); 'I watched a great video yesterday, which demonstrated how to line up the horse for a corner fence' (visual); 'I enjoy grooming my horse' (kinaesthetic). The coach can use this information to get the attention of the rider and stimulate their receptivity to learning. We therefore advocate that the coach employs a range of techniques including diagrams, photographs, demonstrations, metaphors and analogies, music, as well as behaviours, such as 'I *see* what you mean...'; 'I *hear* what you're saying ...'; 'How does your horse *feel* today?', in order to illustrate a learning point.

Questions for coach and learner

Both coach and learner

- What is your own preferred learning style; and that of your learner?

- What learning style might you and they avoid?

- What do you need to unlearn?

- Who else could provide support and challenge?

- What additional resources are needed?

Learner

- What effect did that work have on my colleagues/partnership with my horse?

- What exercises can I take away from the training that will help me to develop my own learning when not supported by my coach?

- How did my coach make me feel (e.g. motivated, empowered to practise on my own, confident, frustrated, demoralised)?

Coach

- To what extent do you adapt your approach according to the learner's preferred style?

- How could you find out the learner's preferred learning style if they are unaware of it?

- What is blocking the learning?

- What can I take from this session to deliver a better session next time?

- What did I learn from the interaction with this person?

- What did I achieve as coach, and was that what the learner expected?

LEARNING

CONTROL VERSUS EMPOWERMENT

There is a safety necessity in riding, which is that the coach maintains the control and confidence of their rider at all times if possible. This has tended to develop a culture in riding coaches wherein 'the coach is always right', and therefore makes all the decisions and maintains complete authority in a training session.

However, this authority takes away any sense of responsibility on the part of the rider. If no decisions have to be made by an individual then, when anything goes wrong, it certainly cannot be their fault! If the coach is completely in control of training content then the rider takes no responsibility for mistakes, but hands that responsibility back to the coach. Mistakes then become the horse's fault or the coach's fault and never the rider's!

The coach has inadvertently allowed a totally 'coach-led' environment to prevail in the sessions (see Scenario 1 below).

It is easy to recognise a rider who has been brought up in this culture. They will always blame the horse for shortcomings. 'He was so tense in the test'; 'I couldn't do anything about it' ; 'He spooked at the flowers'; 'He was stiff and against me all the time.'

▶ EQUESTRIAN SCENARIO 1

The rider trains with her coach three times a week and the horse is ridden in between by the coach. In coaching sessions, whenever there is a problem, the coach rides the horse for the rider and then, when the 'problem' is fixed, the rider is allowed to continue. There is little dialogue between the two while the coach rides the horse, although the coach talks a lot about 'what the rider should be doing'. The sessions are always strongly directed by the coach and rarely is the rider involved in decisions, but the often coach emphasises how well the horse is going when she rides him in between lessons. At a competition, the coach helps the rider to work in, using a two-way radio headset and giving comprehensive information to the rider about what to do whilst warming up. The rider competes and the test has several mistakes, so the rider comes out quite disappointed and is even more upset when she sees her score. The coach debriefs the rider almost as soon as she leaves the arena. There is no feedback from the rider; the coach just tells her all the things that went wrong and what she should have done about them to correct them. The rider disconsolately collects her score sheet and is too disappointed to read it; the coach does not ask to see it and it is lost in the lorry!

▶ EQUESTRIAN SCENARIO 2

The rider has one or two training sessions with his coach each week and, in between, if the rider cannot work the horse, he is hacked or lunged by the rider's mother and is turned out daily. The sessions are directed towards the work the rider identifies that he needs help with. The rider is invited to work in and then give feedback on the initial warm-up, while the coach identifies points of observation. The rider then highlights the area of work they choose to focus on in the session. If the coach feels this is not appropriate, he raises questions to help the rider identify the weaknesses that the coach is seeing. An agreed way forward is decided upon, sharing the rider's feelings and the coach's superior observation, knowledge and experience. The session encourages ongoing feedback from the rider throughout the work, which endorses the rider's knowledge and understanding and enables the coach to know how much the rider is taking in information. The rider is encouraged to discuss the work used in developing the way of going, so that he is aware of which exercises help to improve the horse. At a competition the coach is present, but discusses with the rider the rider's plan before the working in begins. During the working in the rider occasionally rests the horse and, at that point, seeks an opinion from the coach, but more as moral support and reassurance rather than giving controlling instruction. After the test, the rider walks the horse off and is encouraged to think through the test he has ridden, before debriefing with the coach. The debrief involves the rider's feedback first and then, supporting that information, the coach is able to reiterate the strong areas of the test and discuss where some marks might have been lost. The result is then shared by coach and rider and the score sheet becomes a useful tool for further development.

The greatest empowerment a coach can give a rider is to know that they have accumulated tools or strategies to deal with any situation with their horse, through the training sessions. Then, when issues arise at a competition, the rider is independently in control, with techniques to manage those issues. This empowerment is achieved through 'rider-led' sessions, as described in Scenario 2.

The extent to which 'power' is shared between coach and learner, and the range of potential specific coaching styles and behaviours, are outlined in Chapter 6.

'Having trained with Judy Harvey for twenty-three years, I am certainly an advocate of once you find a trainer who suits you, stick with the method and trust your trainer. Certainly Judy's method of training encourages the rider to be able to think for themselves so things don't fall apart when the trainer isn't there. I hope I can convey that to the riders that I now coach.'

RUTH EDGE, international event rider and coach

CRITICAL ANALYSIS

Critical analysis of any process or performance should be useful, but it must be tackled in a sensitive and positive way, and the timing of when to carry out the thorough analysis is also crucial. No one who observed Andy Murray being beaten in a Wimbledon Final and then instantly interviewed on 'how he felt', could fail to sympathise with the intense emotion that he tried desperately to hide. Similarly, a high achievement can generate an intense feeling of relief and emotion following the achievement of a golden goal after months or years of planning.

Critical analysis can fall into several categories:

1. Immediately after the relevant event. This will be charged with the emotion of thc occasion and so is likely to focus on great elation or great despair.

2. After a time of cooling down and relaxation (in equestrian sport, occupied with making sure the horse is comfortable and well managed). Key points may begin to come to focus from the performance.

3. At home in forward planning for the next goal or seasonal plan. It is probably wise to write down an agenda with main points for discussion, to trigger analysis on the past performance and assist in forward planning.

All the points made may apply to a wide range of people such as the rider, parents, coach, friends, groom, and possibly members of the public and officials. In order to conduct the critical analysis, we suggest a structured, planned home meeting led by the rider, with the appropriate people, ideally not too many, allowing plenty of time for a thorough discussion.

CRITICAL ANALYSIS

THE LEARNING JOURNEY

When we consider how, as humans, we become skilful at something, the starting point is that initially something sparks interest – often that is just simple observation. After the London Olympics there was a surge of interest in riding, thanks to the 'dancing horses'. The spectacle of dressage to music changed for a while, from a sport to a vision of loveliness that many people wanted to try for themselves. When we watch any good performance, whatever that might be (top-class ballroom dancing, gym-nastics, ice skating, diving) it looks seamless, effortless and completely harmonious. Watching gives no indication of the blood, sweat and tears involved in reaching that level of competence. When we start a new activ-ity, we are blissfully unaware of how hard it may prove to be. As we proceed, however, we begin a journey that can be described in the following terms.

Unconscious incompetence is the state we are in initially: we don't know what we don't know. After one or two coaching sessions we quickly move to a state of **conscious incompetence**. Here, we are beginning to realise that it is more difficult than it looks, but we are still motivated enough to work at it, knowing what the end aim looks like. This state can last for a long time and can revisit us on many occasions, especially when we don't practise enough, after a lay-off, after an injury, or other mental or physical setback. This state can be with us constantly, albeit at different stages of the activity or sport. It can undermine our confidence and limit our competence and is therefore an area that needs to be managed well by both coach and learner.

As competence develops, we move to a state of **conscious competence.** Now we are realising that all the hard work is beginning to pay off and we know we are gaining in ability. In this state there is still quite a lot of thinking and concentration involved with completing the activity or skill competently. The more practice there is, the better the skill should become, and the need for thinking and concentration diminishes. From this state we eventually move to one of **unconscious competence**, in which we can carry out the activity or skill with a high level of competence, with a seamless and polished appearance that indicates minimal conscious application or thinking. The activity becomes 'automatic'.

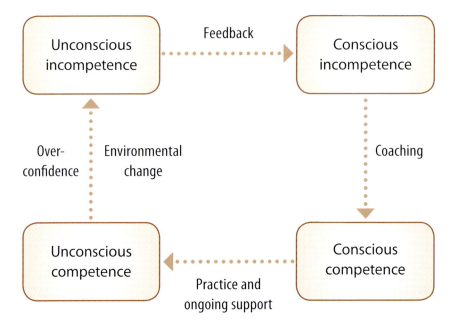

Stages of learning awareness.

To visualise this progression, consider the first time you drove a car and (hopefully) how 'automatically' you now carry out this procedure with minimal actual thought of 'how to do it'.

When preparing for a riding lesson, the coach should consider the rider's awareness of their level of competence. Consider the scenario below.

▶ EQUESTRIAN SCENARIO

Gina has been riding since she was young and has progressed with a pony to achieve a high level of success in dressage, her main interest, at Medium level. She is brave and hard-working. At the age of fifteen she is only 5ft 2in and is very slight in her build; she is intrinsically motivated and, with clear planning and the intention of moving forward in her riding career, a decision is made to sell the pony and find a horse. Gina gets the ride on a big-moving eight-year-old horse that has been trained and produced by her coach who is a professional male rider who is light but nearly 6ft tall. The horse is working at Advanced Medium level and obviously has the ability to be trained further. Gina is in a developmental stage both physically and mentally. She is in the middle of her school GCSE exam year when she first gets the horse to ride and there are many changes happening in her life. She is naturally excited about the prospect of the horse and has glittering aims and aspirations for the future. She has the horse at home and goes to her coach (where the horse was produced) for her lessons. More often than not, when she arrives for her training, her coach says 'Just let me ride him for ten minutes and see how he feels.' The coach then works the horse (usually in silence), then Gina gets on and the session is mostly coach-led, with the coach choosing the work and 'riding the horse from the ground', giving Gina every piece of information in a running commentary of what to do. When she goes home, Gina is finding it increasingly difficult in any way to emulate the work that she sees the coach achieving with the horse. She tries hard to carry out the instructions she has received, but finds that the horse does not feel the same or go the same as he does when she is being supported by her coach. At the next lesson she tries to explain this situation to her coach but her coach just says, 'Don't worry, I'll ride him and put him back together for you.' The process is repeated and the situation has little future.

Let's consider the implications of this scenario in relation to stages of development and also in terms of the coach's role in this situation:

- With her pony (of several years secure, confident relationship) Gina is unconsciously competent. In this state she has time to think about the enjoyment of what she is doing; she can feel confident, positive and in control. All these emotions will give her a good feeling about herself and the pony.

- On her horse, Gina is excited, anticipating great things, aspirational and prepared to work hard. Very quickly, however, she begins to feel at first consciously competent, when she is listening hard to her coach and trying her best to emulate what she sees him doing with the horse. Then, when she gets home, she often moves to being consciously incompetent. This makes her feel that she can't ride anymore; she feels demoralised and frustrated and then the horse seems to go even worse, even though she is 'trying so hard to get it right'.

If we consider the coach and aims of coaching in this situation:

- The coach is probably a very competent rider, and there is little doubt that he considers Gina a capable rider, or he would not have put her on this promising horse.

- He probably feels that, by riding the horse himself when Gina comes for a lesson, he is 'setting the horse up for her'. He is no doubt helping in the short term, but in regard to the longer-term goal of making Gina self-sufficient and able to make the huge change from riding a pony to riding a horse, there is no future in his current plan.

- Gina needs help and support in recognising that the horse is much bigger in size and movement than her pony and has, to date, been ridden by a rider who is much taller, heavier and more experienced than she is. This will hopefully mean that the horse is secure in his work at the current level, but he will have to deal with the huge change to a smaller, lighter, less knowledgeable rider than his initial trainer. This change must be managed in a way by which Gina gains confidence in her ability to ride the horse and is not demoralised by thinking she can't ride anymore.

- The coach, in direct communication with Gina (and possibly a parent), must put together a clear plan to enable Gina to feel she is making steady progress. This requires a programme of work devised through his knowledge of both the horse and Gina, that he knows Gina will be able to cope with at home and feel that she is progressing. At her training sessions he must resist the easy option of getting on the horse and 'showing her how to do it', as this is tending to demoralise Gina, making her think she can't ride the horse as well as her coach does. (That, of course, is true, but it is not helpful to keep highlighting the fact.)

• A good coach will seize the opportunity and take the time to develop the conscious competence of this young rider, so that gradually the horse adapts to the competence of his new rider and a partnership evolves between them. It is likely that there will be a sliding scale of conscious competence, for example in the canter, while unconscious competence has been achieved in walk and trot. As the partnership develops, un-conscious competence may be evident at Medium level while a degree of conscious competence is still needed in setting up flying changes at Advanced Medium level.

• The coach needs to consider how he can best help Gina to manage the change from pony to horse. His skill as a rider is not in question as he has trained the horse well, but now he must show equal skill in coaching the rider, to make a partnership with the well-trained horse. He must try to put himself into Gina's shoes and relate to the feeling of conscious incompetence. He must then develop the skills to help her move from conscious competence to unconscious competence.

BELIEFS, ATTITUDES AND MINDSETS

In exploring the subject of this chapter, which is about 'thinking', we need to consider beliefs, attitudes and mindset, as these all influence our behav-iour. In some cases we have inherited these from others – parents, guard-ians, teachers. If these have been absorbed without question, they may be less useful to us, given our personal context and reality. For example, if an individual has been influenced by another with the statement 'women are easier to work with than men', this over-generalised statement would not reflect everyone's experience and would be unhelpful if someone worked in a totally male environment.

 Mindset is the basic state of mind or way of thinking, from which evolves attitudes expressed as our manner, feelings, thoughts and behaviours, which others see and react to. Horses certainly have 'attitude' on occasion and, if that meets the attitude of a rider 'head-on', the result may be interesting or challenging to the coach!

Coaches need to appreciate how the learner thinks, and what internal drivers are present – values inform beliefs, attitudes and mindsets and these, in turn, shape assumptions. Assumptions underpin behaviour, and all behaviour should be goal-driven. The coach and learner need to make these connections – for example, if a person's belief system included: 'everyone is guilty until proven innocent', then their behaviour would be very different from another individual who held the opposite belief: 'innocent until proven guilty.'

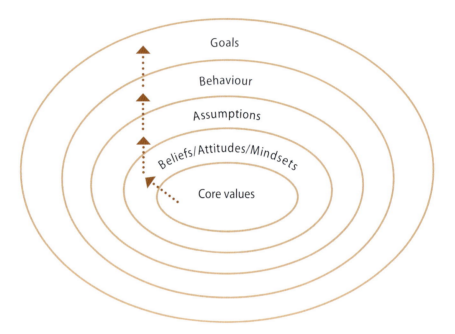

Elements of personality.

Here is an example of the 'knock-on' influence of an underlying value:

Value: All horses should be treated with dignity.

Belief/Attitude/Mindset: One should be a conscientious horse owner.

Assumption: Horses will perform better if they are treated well.

Behaviour: The horse is given a varied life, for example, turnout in the field, hacks, and schooling, with the appropriate levels of exercise and the right type of feed relevant to the required performance.

Goal: A happy, safe horse.

However, the following beliefs would limit learning, riding and competition opportunities:

'All stallions are dangerous' (some are, some aren't).

'Chestnut mares are always difficult' (possible, but not guaranteed).

'My team-mate is older than me and therefore has more experience' (the colleague may have repeated the same experience many times and therefore *not* have depth and breadth of experience).

Regarding the above, the coach could offer an alternative view, such as: 'Mares can be cooperative and brave, especially on the polo field'; or share a different experience such as: 'I competed a stallion for many years who was easy to handle, even around mares'.

BLINKERED VIEW

▶CORPORATE SCENARIO

Jonathan is a senior partner in a law firm. Client feedback has recently indicated some dissatisfaction with the service they are receiving, mainly because of the high turnover of staff on the client account team. Following a number of team meetings, it became clear that morale was low. On further investigation, some employees made the following comments: 'We are only ever criticised for our work with the client – never praised', and, 'Work has become so serious and dull that we're less motivated.' Jonathan thought he had a large group of self-starters, so was initially annoyed by the feedback. However, following an intensive discussion with an executive coach, he identified a significant personal insight – Jonathan's belief and mindset was: 'No gain without pain'. The resulting behaviour was to push his team too hard, and if they reached the standards and objectives set by him, his response was to think that he must have set the bar too low. The team wanted and valued honest feedback, but the absence of any appreciation resulted in transfers to other departments where there was a culture of 'serious endeavour with enjoyment'. Although Jonathan had lost some valuable specialists, he was able to stop the flow of exits from the team by changing his leadership style to include more personal connection with individuals, encouragement, thank-yous and rewards such as dinners to celebrate successful projects delivered to the client.

Attitude, feelings and thoughts can be affected by so many circumstances, for example:

- An unkind remark from a 'friend' or sibling.

- A misunderstanding or misheard remark from a coach/parent/partner. For example: 'I heard him say my new horse wasn't up to much.'

- A perceived manner or observed body language from a significant other. For example: 'I walked past and s/he ignored me.'

(The implications of how negative beliefs about oneself will limit a person from being at their best will be highlighted in Chapter 4.)

The learner's way of behaving or reacting may relate to circumstances of which the coach is unaware. Communication is always the key to understanding a perceived attitude.

Potential coaching solutions

If faced with the above, there are a number of solutions that the coach could employ:

- Coaches need to bring a positive mindset themselves, based on what's possible rather than what's not.

- The approach between the coach and learner should be collaborative, and create an environment in which both parties can think in a co-creative way, looking for innovative solutions to old problems and/or new challenges.

- Both parties need to understand that there is no one 'best way' that fits all situations.

- A coach should tactfully and carefully probe the situation with sensitive questions, ensuring that they 'read' the answers carefully, without exacerbating the issue by a tactless 'What's your problem?' sort of enquiry! For example, it may be that a rider has had a grim day with a horse pulling a shoe off, the farrier not turning up as arranged, getting stuck in traffic on their way to the lesson and arriving having forgotten to bring the horse's brushing boots. One of 'those days', when everything conspires against the rider, will not put them in a good frame of mind.

- The learner may need to be challenged if they have limiting beliefs, an unconscious bias and/or assumptions that have not been tested.

- The skill of the coach is to recognise potentially limiting beliefs, attitudes and mindsets and, if need be, adapt their coaching style in order to shift these to more helpful and positive ones. Different coaching approaches and styles will be discussed more fully in Chapter 6.

- The coach needs to be aware of the learner's overall mindset to learning – is it a growth mindset or closed mindset? If it is the latter, this would need to be shifted first in order to gain the maximum benefit from the experience.

> 'There is a big difference between being a trainer and being a coach. Knowing when to switch from being one to being the other is an important key to getting the best from riders.'
>
> **CHRIS BARTLE FBHS,**
> international rider and coach, trainer of the German Olympic eventing team

BARRIERS TO LEARNING

There may be many reasons why an individual is resistant to learning. These could be external factors such as geography and/or intrapersonal issues such as a history of negative learning experiences.

Location may also be a barrier – for example, a rider may need to travel a long way to work with their coach. It would be useful to be aware of the camps and clinics run by organisations such as the equestrian disciplines, as these can provide an excellent training immersion, and compliment individual coaching sessions. The coach should encourage the rider to look for clinics near their yard, with visiting coaches, and be open to supporting these.

Lack of time could be an issue. It can be motivational and informative to watch other riders being coached, which might be less time-consuming and expensive for some people than transporting their own horse. Also, the perception of 'time' may need to be reframed – impactful coaching should reduce the number of competitions that a rider would need to do in order to qualify for a championship, thereby saving time.

Financial constraints may impact significantly on how much coaching a rider can engage in. Fees vary considerably depending on the knowledge, experience and reputation of the coach. Some coaches may also charge for their petrol if they are making a special visit for just one person. Shared sessions may need to be offered, in order to spread the fee for the rider. However, although financial constraints may be entirely genuine, it is fundamentally more useful to view coaching as an investment rather than a cost.

Personal blocks such as fear of failure are not uncommon, and may show up in different ways, for example, avoiding competing at a higher level, unexpected 'illness' on the day of competition, avoidance tactics prior to an important competition, excuses for not competing. We will discuss this fear, and other types of concerns, in more detail in Chapter 4.

Surprisingly in equestrian sport, one of the biggest barriers to learning, that one would least expect or identify with, is the parents of a young rider. Ask any sportsperson and they will tell you what that road to success really looks like.

Many parents are in a position to make life much easier for their children than they themselves experienced when growing up. It is human nature to want to give to your children and to help them avoid the pitfalls and bad experiences that life throws at you. However, to overprotect them from these experiences is a huge barrier to *their* learning, *their* development and ultimately *their* success.

Watch a tiny child who is learning to crawl. What motivates them? In one word: *curiosity*. It is curiosity about what is on the other side of the room, what the remote control handset (which is five feet away from them) feels like, what they can see out of the window. It is curiosity that intrinsically motivates them to strive (to crawl). If everything is provided within their reach instantly, why the need to crawl to reach it?

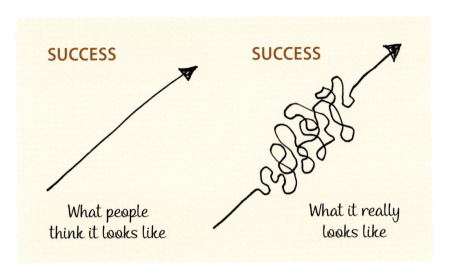

SUCCESS · SUCCESS

What people think it looks like · What it really looks like

The road to success.

If you take away that curiosity and that need to strive – for example, by providing all that a young rider needs (the best horse, the best coach, the best environment, with no pressure of looking after the horse themselves or getting up in the small hours to tack up and ride before school) – you are gradually taking away that intrinsic motivation and, when that rider fails to achieve, then the excuses will be put in place. (The judge didn't like them, the horse was a bit fresh and there was not enough time to work in as we got stuck in traffic, the rider has had a tough week at school, etc.). While it is a huge asset for any competitor to have a support system that seeks to mini-mise or alleviate obstacles, they still need to have a fundamental, intrinsic motivation to self-start, and that motivator must be recognised by the coach and nurtured between competitor and coach.

Consider: 'Don't worry darling, you will never have to ride this horse again, I will make sure you have a better one!' Delivered by a parent after a bad performance, what message is this sending out to the rider? It is saying: 'It's not your fault, lay the blame elsewhere.'

If the parent has been very successful in the same sport, whatever that may be, then the offspring may be striving not to let the parent down. This can be positive and motivational to an extent, but the parent needs to be sensitive to the expectations of the youngster and ensure that there is no adverse pressure put on them. The young person must not see themselves as letting down the parent if they are not successful.

ROLE MODELS

As discussed in learning styles, one of the ways we learn is 'visually' and, if one looks at many instances of wild animal behaviour, animals mimic or copy behaviour. Ask most people whether they have a role model and the majority will give a name of a well-known person whom they admire. If you are speaking to a person involved in equestrian sport, then they will usually refer to the top names featuring at the highest level in the sport currently. If you refer to tennis, particularly in June, most people will identify one of the seeded players at Wimbledon. If you direct a learner's thinking towards a world figure, they will often come up with names like HM Queen Elizabeth, Nelson Mandela, Mother Teresa of Calcutta or even Princess Diana.

When questioned further as to why the named person is admired and regarded as a role model, there may be various reasons given. It may be the characteristics of personality that are considered of value; it may be what they have achieved in their particular field; it may perhaps be the first 'famous' person who came to mind. Whatever the reason for the name, that person has impacted on the individual's mind and created either interest or motivation. That word 'curiosity' comes up again – curiosity about the role model's ability, training, commitment, method of achieving success: a belief that 'If they can do it then maybe so can I'.

After any high-achieving success in sport there is usually a surge in interest in that sport, through the publicity radiated by the winning individual, recent examples being cyclists Bradley Wiggins and Chris Froome (winning the Tour de France) and Andy Murray (winning Wimbledon) for tennis. This shows just how strongly role models can influence the enthusiasm for sport, even though this can often have only the 'mushroom effect' – a sudden rush of growth followed by an inevitable fading again as the impact of the winner moves out of the public eye. If, however, a coach can utilise a role model effectively, then it is a way of structuring a learner's development and using the role model to re-motivate the learner on occasions when intrinsic drive is low. How often have you been to a competition as a spectator, only to return thoroughly inspired and with a renewed drive to train harder, practise more and believe that you can achieve your next goal?

In the case just cited we are considering role models as always having a positive influence on our learning, but bad examples can also be used as models of learning. As coaches we should encourage our learners not only to be as good as they can be, but also to win and lose with fairness and grace.

There will be instances when we observe bad sportsmanship and ungracious behaviour. Even though justification may be offered by those present ('They were so upset at being beaten – that's why they reacted as they did'; 'They only said that in the heat of the moment having just lost that really important game') there is, in fact, never an excuse for this.

INSIGHTS

- Transformational and sustainable change is more likely to occur following the approach outlined in 'Equestrian Scenario 2' (see pages 77–8). The overall aim would be to help the learner become more self-managing and inter-dependent.

- It takes time to master any skill and arrive in the state of unconscious competence.

- A learner-led approach is more likely than a coach-led one to engage the learner and increase their commitment to the learning process.

- A good equestrian coach will always be aware of the competence level of their rider in any given situation. This must never be *assumed* and often the key to finding out the rider's level of competence is by one or two well-timed questions.

- There should be an awareness that age, educational level, cultural background and motivation will influence an individual's approach to learning.

- Coaches should plan to use a variety of delivery methods to allow learners to experience a range of learning approaches.

- We all naturally engage in the learning cycle outlined on pages 74–5, however, we all have a preferred style.

- Sensitivity in how the coach assesses the attitude of the learner and manages it, can influence whether the subsequent session is positive or adds to the learner's list of factors creating a 'bad day'.

- Experience is not what happens to you, it's what you learn and how you use that experience to further your learning.

4. EMOTIONAL

POINT OF VIEW

In order to release surprising potential, a coach needs to understand their own and their learner's emotional process. Our feelings can help or hinder our progress – we therefore should explore, understand and manage our emotions.

In the previous chapter we dealt with the first of the two intertwined elements of psychology: *thinking*. We now address the second: *feeling*.

This chapter will explore the consequences of negative and positive belief cycles and how these can be interrupted or enhanced. It will also highlight the emotions that can be triggered when individuals are faced with personal change and pressure.

> 'To be a good coach technical knowledge is essential, championship athletes have one common thread, the desire for more knowledge. To be a great coach you need to be able to manage your character and that of the athletes on the coal face when under fire. Technical knowledge will get you there, managing character will win medals.'
>
> **MAJOR R.G. WAYGOOD MBE,** Chef d'Equipe, GBR dressage team

MANAGING EXTERNAL INFLUENCES AND PRESSURES

In sport – and particularly in equestrian sport – there are many instances where external influences and pressures create a block to the natural progress of development that would proceed more easily if no influences or pressures arose. The list is endless but could include the following:

Coach

- Domestic issues that disturb your role and cause you to have undue worry, stress, fatigue and resulting lack of health and well-being.

- Taking on too much work and trying to fulfil a role for all your learners.

- Antagonism between you and your learner, or their significant others.

- Financial worries.

- High expectation of your learner, which is not fulfilled. If there are poor results, who is at fault?

Learner

- Pressure from work or education that disturbs the training process.

- Pressure from significant others (parents, sponsor) to achieve and not being able to fulfil this.

- Financial constraints (cost of training, competing, running the lorry, etc.)

- Pressure from peer group (if aiming for a team place) – with adolescents, often internal pressure from team-mates, parents and others.

The most important factor in any situation where there may be external pressures and influences, is to identify these at the earliest opportunity and be able to bring them into the open. Communication and discussion can then be employed to develop a manageable strategy to try to deal with the issue(s) and provide a solution that can bring about a reduction of the problem. 'A problem shared is a problem halved' and 'There is no such thing as a problem, only a solution' are valuable and well-used sayings, even though the response to both could just as swiftly be: 'Easier said than done'.

Certainly, if external influences and pressures are not managed, then the outcome is likely to be a demoralised learner or a coach under pressure, and the ultimate outcome in an equestrian scenario is that the horse/rider relationship suffers. Remember, the horse lives in the moment, he has no external influences and pressures unless they arise 'in the moment'. A bird flies out of the hedge and it frightens him, because he is taken by surprise at that moment, but he never worries about whether he has enough money in his bank account to buy his next set of shoes! That is our worry and we must manage it.

Where does one begin on this subject? With the rider alone the list can be lengthy, but when the horse is added in, it can become endless. It is a subject that needs due consideration by both coach and rider, because of the huge influence it may have on careful planning. It will overlap with dealing with success and failure, which will also be discussed in this chapter.

▶ EQUESTRIAN SCENARIO

Alex has fulfilled all the criteria required to put her in line for a place on the European Championship team for ponies. At the final trial there is a decision to measure ponies as this will happen at the Europeans. Alex's pony measures 1cm too big. The selectors cannot take the risk in taking the partnership to the Europeans and then having the pony 'measured out' and eliminated from the competition. Alex is told that she will no longer be in contention for selection.

Within half a day the circumstances have changed from:

- Excited, positive rider looking forward to the day and beyond to a team place.

- Supportive, proud parents who have worked hard all season to date to ensure that Alex is in the best place to fulfil requirements for team selection.

- Coach who has worked with the rider to plan and prepare for every eventuality and left no stone unturned to aid progress to this seasonal 'golden goal'.

- High expectations of significant others (e.g. grandparents, siblings, friends, supporters, local sponsors, owner of the pony if not in the ownership of Alex's family).

To:

- Devastated rider, as she sees her achievement snatched away from her (and her role given to someone else).

- Devastated parents who are likely to react strongly and often with intense anger at the apparent injustice of the situation, coupled with not being able to control the situation in any way. Seeing the disappointment of their daughter is a powerful motivator to bring out the protective mechanism to limit the pain that the child is suffering.

- For the coach, intense personal disappointment for their pupil where there have been months of preparation involved in coming to this point.

- Bemusement and lack of understanding from all the significant others, who will then begin to react themselves, depending on the information that they receive from the situation. They may become strong allies to the parents who are planning to complain to anyone who will listen.

This is just one example of how circumstances can change in a moment. The managing strategies required (which in this case would probably have to be led by the coach), are essential in the damage limitation of an immediate crisis like this. Potential coaching solutions may be along the following lines:

- Someone must take control. The first consideration must be for the devastated rider.

- Take the rider somewhere private (a horsebox is probably ideal) and, if necessary, suggest that the parents go and put the pony away, or deploy them in a way that keeps them 'doing something'. They will be experiencing their own 'meltdown' feelings and these will be different from those of the rider. If the parents insist on being present, then be aware of the intensity of the feelings they will be having in wanting to protect their child from the pain.

- Deal with these kind of situations with quick thinking, tact, authority, sympathy, listening, understanding and decision-making in the short term. Then use many of these qualities in the follow-up days to rebuild goals and confidence.

PERSONAL BLOCKS

In order to enhance our performance, we can develop a great plan, invest in lots of preparation, engage in training and receive support, but find that 'on the day' something gets in the way of us delivering to our desired standard. This block may only happen occasionally when certain dynamics, negative beliefs and feelings are at play. We all experience personal blocks regardless of our role, age or position in life. Personal blocks for both coaches and learners will limit progress and occasionally stop them from performing at their best.

Blocks can be seen in the following loose categories, which overlap and intertwine with each other:

- Deviant manifestations of overused strengths, for example, a brave rider who pushes their horse too much.

- Fear-based driven behaviour, for example, a learner who is too cautious.

- Negative beliefs that engage learners in self-defeating behaviour, for example, a person who avoids asking a coach to change their style.

One way of identifying that a block has been triggered is to notice patterns of behaviour resulting in a predictable outcome, over which the person feels they have no control!

Critical incidents and overused strengths

Generally, we bring our best intentions and skills to our day-to-day life. We are conscious of our responsibilities and opportunities, and know that we have to stretch ourselves in order to accomplish what we and others need from us. This stretch can often contain the seeds of a learner's vulnerability. It seems natural that 'stretch' should mean that a learner does more of what they already do well now, to amplify their strength to a new level. Often, unfortunately, this leads to the overuse of a strength, tipping normally useful, purposeful behaviour into self-defeating and driven action with the consequent negative outcomes for the individual, and horse, and sometimes those around them.

It is precisely at the moment when a strength is needed that it can be overused in volume and intensity. These will be moments when the consequences of continued exploitation, inertia or failure will be at their highest and the resultant pressure or stress will be more likely to affect the judgement of the coach and/or learner. In this way, for example, the wonderful gift of plain-speaking can tip over into cruelty or bullying; the enabling capacity to collaborate can turn to semi-cringing appeasement; the purposeful driving force of passion can become a frenzy of contradictory energy and effort.

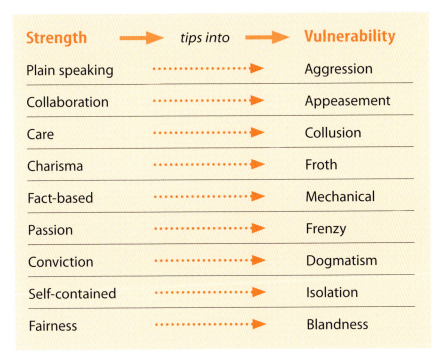

Strength	tips into	Vulnerability
Plain speaking	┈┈▶	Aggression
Collaboration	┈┈▶	Appeasement
Care	┈┈▶	Collusion
Charisma	┈┈▶	Froth
Fact-based	┈┈▶	Mechanical
Passion	┈┈▶	Frenzy
Conviction	┈┈▶	Dogmatism
Self-contained	┈┈▶	Isolation
Fairness	┈┈▶	Blandness

Examples of overused strengths.

For someone to recalibrate their strengths means they are adjusting, re-generating their sense of self; their identity. This will mean examining their reflex instincts, their seemingly natural uncontrolled reactions, when under pressure in stressful situations. This can be daunting, as it is about unpicking what is, in one sense, a very useful and comfortable garment: their strengths. However, as long as a learner chooses to engage with others in worthwhile endeavour they will meet defining moments.

Fear-based, driven behaviour

At the root of an individual's personal identity is a needs-based guidance system that, when working at its best, leads them toward satisfying their needs and away from the negative consequences of not meeting their needs. Some of these negative consequences will be emotional, and moving away from these emotions can become a need in its own right.

So, rather than just fearing the negative emotion that will occur when a need is not met, the fear of the negative emotion becomes a motivator – whether a need is there or not. For example, the motivation moves from eating in order to gain sustainable nourishment to eating because we are fearful about being hungry. This is, of course, more likely to lead to overeating.

These concerns, fears and disabling worries come from early breakdowns in our personal and social development. This leads to seemingly irrational fears which, as the pattern unfolds, guarantee that we end up in the condition our behaviour is trying to protect us from.

Realistic fears and concerns are absolutely essential to keep us safe as we move forward in life. However, if they start to engage self-defeating behaviour they need examination and action. An enlightened coach will be aware of, and challenge, their own fears, and can play a powerful part in helping the learner overcome theirs.

A fear of failure *can* lead us to achieve but, if unchecked, can lead to setting only incremental goals which never really satisfy. A concern over intimacy can lead to real loneliness. A questioning stance on how authority is used can lead either to healthy interdependence or rebellion. The tipping point will again occur in certain situations; defining moments, when the stress perceived moves the behaviour from rational concern over reaching a goal, to a real fear that makes us move clumsily away from an imagined, amplified, threat. Again, there is the possibility of a double negative here as it is not just the fear of *being foolish*, for example, but the fear of *being seen to*

Fear of *drives a*	Positive outcome	*but can also lead to* Negative outcome
Failure	Success	Unsatisfying goals
Being foolish	Respect	Loss of dignity
Intimacy	Rugged individualism	Loneliness
Authority figures	Interdependence	Co- or Counter-dependence
Rejection	Acceptance	Isolation
Conflict	Harmony	Disconnection
Ambiguity	Clarity	Confusion

Fear-based blocks.

be foolish that is the trigger. The consequent negative judgement we expect from others that flows from being 'caught in the act' adds a layer of shame.

If a coach has a fear of conflict, then they may not take a stand with an aggressive parent. If a learner has a discomfort with intimacy, then they may not disclose personal problems which are impacting on their performance. If the learner has a block in relation to authority figures then they could 'go along' with a coach even if they feel let down.

Negative belief cycles

A further way of understanding how learners block themselves from being the best they can become, is that they sometimes choose not to examine the negative beliefs they hold about themselves and the consequences of their behaviour which click into place when they feel under stress.

These negative beliefs, and resultant self-defeating behaviours, are individualised and each person will have their own distinct pattern of stopping themselves getting what they need and want. So, a coach might have the negative belief that, if they express excitement, learners won't take them seriously. This will lead to a mindset of emotional caution, which will

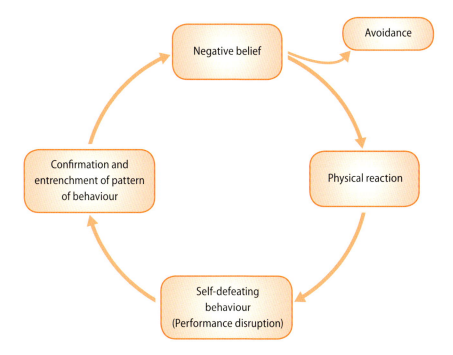

The generalised negative cycle.

lead to the stilted, flat presentation of an idea, which the learner therefore doesn't take seriously. Another coach or learner may have a negative belief that, if they are serious, other people won't enjoy being with them. This, under stress, leads to a mindset of convivial banter, which leads to seemingly frivolous attention to important matters and, in consequence, the learner doesn't learn.

▶EQUESTRIAN SCENARIO

Jack is a strong, no-nonsense coach who specialises in showjumping. Part of his credibility comes from his past success as a rider, and his reputation for running challenging clinics. Jack is well-intentioned and wants the best for his clients. He is happy to work with riders at different levels, on different types of horses, but prefers students who are competitively ambitious. His clinics are well attended by riders, who come on a regular basis. Jack has a fear of failure, as he didn't do well at school with his basic education and therefore feels that he has something to prove to the world. He has very high standards for himself, and for others, which leads to his coaching style being rather pushy – whilst at the same time, taking too much responsibility for the rider's learning. He can get stuck in the negative belief cycle illustrated below.

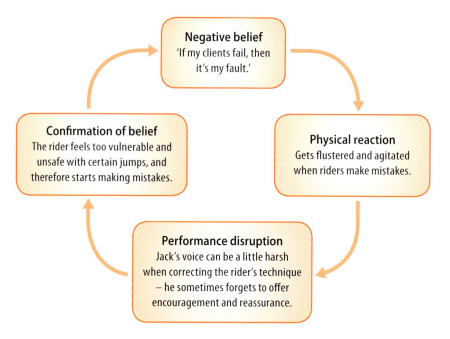

Jack's negative belief cycle.

One of his pupils is Ian – they have been working together for a couple of months, once or twice a week. Ian is a good rider but lacks confidence at shows. Jumping is his hobby, but he hopes to go as far as he can, so is an active competitor with two horses. He has just bought a new horse that is only six and a little green in relation to jumping, but has a lot of potential. The horse has a scopey jump, and can already 'turn on a sixpence', but is quite strong. Ian feels safer when competing indoors rather than outdoors. Ian has a fear of conflict as he often backs down when there is even the slightest hint of a disagreement. Ian's parents are both academics, and meals in their household in the past, involved 'robust' debate. Along with three loud older brothers, Ian found that environment rather intimidating. Ian's negative belief cycle can play out in the way illustrated.

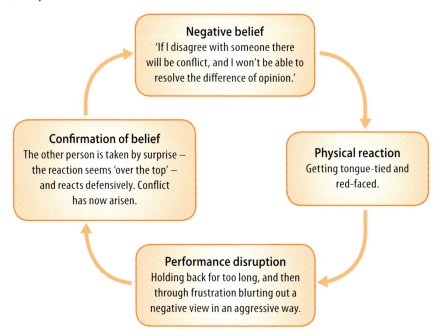

Ian's negative belief cycle.

Recently, Jack's and Ian's negative belief cycles clashed …

They had been taking things carefully with the new horse – who was responding well. However, in the last coaching session, Jack suggested they work outdoors. Ian was a little nervous about this, but said nothing. The horse reacted well to the trotting poles and the first few small jumps, but the local farmer decided to move some cows into the neighbouring field during the lesson. The horse was a little distracted (although not spooky) but Ian would have preferred to stop jumping until the manoeuvre was over, but again said nothing. Jack told Ian to take another fence … Ian wanted to refocus the horse away from the cows but used too much leg, so the horse got stronger and rushed the fence. Given the tension and lack of balance in the approach, the horse missed his stride and put in a huge 'green' jump, so Ian fell off. He and the horse were not hurt, but Ian was angry. He got hold of the horse and walked out of the arena, saying that the incident was Jack's fault. The atmosphere was now thick with tension … neither party was sure how to proceed. Jack was blaming himself for telling Ian to 'get a grip' and Ian was unable to express his concerns in an assertive rather than aggressive manner. Both parties were now feeling at best confused, at worst frustrated, with their communication in breakdown.

In such a scenario, ideally, the two parties would need to talk through what had happened, and be honest about the contribution they both made to the situation. There would need to be a willingness to acknowledge and discuss their feelings, and be open about why they felt the way they did.

Negative belief cycles can be triggered regardless of our role(s) in life, as shown below.

▶ CORPORATE SCENARIO 1

Joanne works for a marketing and advertising consultancy. She is technically very competent and has come up through the ranks within her existing organisation – she therefore understands their systems and procedures well. Joanne's creativity has helped shape many successful marketing campaigns for their clients. A promotion opportunity has recently emerged … if successful, she would move from being a consultant generating ideas and concepts, to a client account management role. This would entail leadership, personnel management and business development. Outside of work, Joanne is seen as the 'life and soul of the party' amongst her friends, but at work she has a professional façade, which is only lowered or softened once she has known people for some time. Her colleagues sometimes refer to her as the 'Ice Queen'. Joanne has a fear of intimacy, and is therefore reluctant to disclose personal matters with people she knows less well. Therefore, with this cool demeanour, others are less likely to talk to her about themselves, so it is sometimes difficult to develop personal connections with clients. Successful business development would be dependent to some extent on her ability to build strong, trustful relationships with existing and potential clients. Joanne understands that she needs to show more vulnerability, and engage in a wider range of conversations, not just those relating to tasks, campaigns and budgets. To break out of this negative cycle, Joanne needs to trust others more, and show genuine interest in her clients' personal as well as business agendas. She has decided to talk through her concerns with friends as they have some understanding about where the fear has come from, in that she felt badly let down by a previous boyfriend. She hopes that they can help her see that the 'past is the past'. She has also requested the opportunity to shadow her employer's most successful client account manager, who excels in winning new business by building high-value relationships. Joanne therefore hopes to break out of the cycle illustrated.

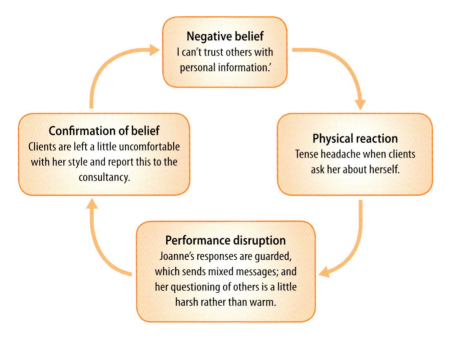

Joanne's negative belief cycle.

▶ CORPORATE SCENARIO 2

Andrew works as a sales representative for a leading car manufacturer. He enjoys the variety in his work and meeting different types of customers. The atmosphere in the car showroom is relaxed most of the time, however, there is sometimes competitive tension between the sales team members. They have all been given stretching targets and, whilst the manufacturer they represent is popular, there are organisational blocks which can get in the way of a successful sale, such as the reception staff not taking down the correct contact details when a potential customer phones, looking for more information on a car and expecting a sales person to call them back. Andrew knows that the initial point of contact is important and, if a good first impression has been created, it's likely that the customer will ask for that salesperson again, should they wish to place an order. Andrew was promised a bonus (10 per cent of his salary) after twelve months if he achieved all his targets. He has succeeded in meeting 80 per cent of his objectives, but the company is only going to give him a 5 per cent increase. Nine times out of ten, when he has full access to a potential customer, this leads to a sale. However, as an enthusiastic and willing employee, he gets asked to help out with many activities that are not always sales related. So, he can be dealing with a potential purchaser but be called away … in which case a sales colleague may continue with the client, take an order and claim full responsibility for their success.

Negative belief
'It's not my place to challenge those in authority. They have more experience than me and therefore know better.'

Confirmation of belief
The manager dismisses Andrew's concerns and closes the meeting by saying that the situation won't change for as long as Andrew is viewed as a 'junior' member of staff.

Physical reaction
Andrew is concerned about the meeting and so missed breakfast – this has made him a little light-headed. He also didn't sleep well in anticipation of the discussion, and is therefore tired.

Performance disruption
Andrew is in two minds whether or not to cancel the meeting with his manager. Having dithered, he ends up being a few minutes late. In the meeting, his views are not backed up with reasons, and his voice has little conviction. All of the above do not leave the manager with a favourable impression.

Andrew's negative belief cycle.

Andrew would like to stay with his employer, but feels that their system is sometimes unfair, especially as he is allocated Saturdays in his shift less often than his colleagues. This is a popular day for buyers so, having seen his schedule for the following month, Andrew decides that he must talk with his manager. Unfortunately, Andrew has a fear of authority, so he is nervous about the meeting. His negative belief cycle would usually transpire as shown in the illustration on the page opposite.

Breaking through personal blocks

The ways out of these block cycles are similar to those already discussed. First, you can choose not to enter the cycle and therefore avoid the pressure. This won't be the best choice for any regenerative change cycle you are engaged in, as the block will not go away, and change necessarily provokes pressure and stress. The other options are to prepare and rehearse different behavioural choices, to imagine more positive outcomes, to reframe the disabling mindsets, and be prepared to take calculated risks. Replacing 'I can't win' with 'I always win' is just as far-fetched but much more motivating. However, just recognising the cycle in itself may encourage the individual to stop avoiding difficult scenarios and practise more helpful strategies. Susan Jeffers' book: *Feel the Fear and Do it Anyway* outlines this approach. Creating useful experiments in safe, low-risk situations can increase confidence, and facilitate breakthroughs. Another technique is 'reframing', which is taken from Neuro-Linguistic Programming (NLP). This is an approach to communication, personal development and psychotherapy created by Richard Bandler and John Grinder in California in the 1990s. See pages 115–17 for examples of how reframing can be used to create more positive thoughts and feelings.

THE TRANSITION CURVE

Learning requires change and this will provoke a range of emotions, regardless of whether the change is imposed, or initiated, and whether it is perceived as negative or positive. Kubler-Ross's research in 1991 identified that our human responses and feelings will be different depending on where we are in the transition curve (see diagram below).

- **Denial** This initial stage is when we grapple to accept the reality of the situation/information: 'Will this actually happen?' 'Do I want it to happen?' 'Can I cope with it happening?' 'Should I perhaps pretend it is not really happening?'

- **Blaming self** As we continue to move on we may find ourselves feeling more and more that 'It's my fault – of course it's not their fault'; 'It's really me – how dreadful, what an awful person I am ...'

- **Blaming others** As we move from denial to acceptance it is easy to blame others for the pain/discomfort we are starting to experience – 'It's all their fault.'

- **Confusion** The feeling most normally associated with 'acceptance' – often the most unnerving place to be but the one that appears necessary before real change can start to happen.

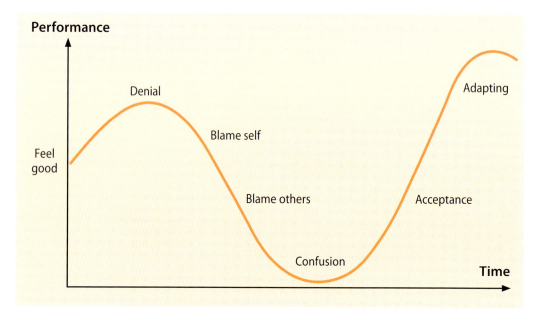

Transition curve.

- **Acceptance** Often a very low period, when the full impact of change is acknowledged and we are in the middle of our fears or frustrations in trying to solve matters.

- **Adaptation** The stage where our problem-solving skills have started to work and we begin to move towards the new situation by integrating new behaviours.

It is natural and useful to move through all these stages – it might take a few minutes if, for example, we lose our car keys – or years, particularly if we get stuck in one type of response. There have been sad cases of employees being made redundant but still dressing for work each day and standing by the gates of their previous employer. Coaches can play an important role in encouraging the learner to 'move on'. This could be done by reassuring the learner that taking the next step will be 'okay'; inviting them to talk with others who've had similar experiences in the past and to learn successfully from them; and/or providing different perspectives on the same situation or issue. Navigating a successful transition through these emotions should lead to the learner feeling and being in a better place, for example, more confident and/or competent than at the beginning of the change.

DEALING WITH EXPECTATION, DISAPPOINTMENT AND SUCCESS

Managing disappointment

If your goal is perfection, then you will always experience some level of disappointment, especially in the equestrian world. (Perfection is unattainable with horses, except for the briefest moment, which serves to instil frustration in the perfectionist, as that glimpse of what they aim for flits tantalisingly in and out.)

Disappointment is fundamental to sport and to life, because it is the defeat of one's hopes and expectations. We experience it throughout our life at varying levels, it being intrinsic to life. Coupled with disappointment will be words like 'effort' and 'preparation', often involving large investments in time, training and accompanying financial cost. Effort and preparation, anticipation and hope, will almost certainly all be the forerunners to success or failure.

The preparation, which leads to expectation, will probably have included:

- Planning (maybe over years, certainly involving months).
- Goal-setting.
- Practice.
- Reviewing.
- Reflecting.
- Adjusting goals based on results, review and reflection.
- Time.
- Money.
- Commitment.
- Effort (from the rider, coach and significant others).

Along with various other factors.

Now consider who will be affected by the disappointment:

- Primarily the rider – who *owns* the disappointment!
- The coach.
- Partner.
- Parents.
- Friends, colleagues (at school or work).
- Other members of the family.
- The owner of the horse.
- Possibly others: sponsors, selectors, team-mates.
- Peripheral others (press, social media forums, etc.).

If the disappointment is the primary 'possession' of the rider, then consider for a moment the implications there are, when several other people (some of them very influential to the rider, either emotionally in the rider's life or from a sport development viewpoint) are involved and try to share the disappointment. The extent to which the different individuals involved will feel the disappointment will be dependent on:

- Why they feel it.

- How much they hold themselves responsible for it. For example, the coach may feel that they have not prepared the rider sufficiently for success.

- How much others want to protect the rider from it.

- Whether or not the disappointment is relevant to the future plan. Missing a possible long-list or selection for a team place could be an important result which impacts negatively on a number of people (selector/owner/sponsor).

- Whether it brings into question the competence of the rider, which may influence a judgement on the horse's future with this rider (sponsor, owner, World Class Development Programme).

Taking all this into consideration, the primary pain and disappointment still 'belong' to the rider; it is theirs to manage and deal with, and the reaction of others involved may only serve to concentrate and compound the pain and dismay the rider is feeling.

Consider these revealing statements:

- 'When I don't get a good score my mother is so upset that I feel like a double failure for making her so disappointed.'

- 'When I don't do well, my dad says "Couldn't you have tried harder; you've got a better horse than all the other riders I watched and you are certainly better than the one who beat you."'

Remember that the lack of achievement is felt most strongly by the rider, and they must be able to take the lead on how they deal with the disappointment. Younger riders, in particular, may need guidance with how to process it.

Disappointment can be a totally negative influence if handled consistently badly, or it can be 'managed' into a constructive critical analysis (see page 78).

- Allow the rider the freedom to 'fail', 'under-perform' or 'have a bad day'.

- Encourage them to self-reflect in their own time.

- Consider what went wrong, why it went wrong and, if given the opportunity to have an 'instant replay' of their performance, what they would do differently.

- All of these points relate equally to the coach as to the rider.

- Reflection may be relevant to adjusting a goal and changing or further developing the training.

- How often do we hear: 'I wish I'd done ...' This is hindsight, but it can be extremely valid and a strong coaching tool. Learning by experience (as already discussed) is a one of the strongest means of confirming feeling, effect or control.

- As the coach, redefine success clearly. First place is not the only way to be successful.

- Allow the rider to develop the ability to define progress by the pathway of development (not only the winning performances).

- Encourage the rider to look at role models (see page 90) who have turned disappointment into success.

There must therefore be some rewards in managing disappointment. These may include:

- It builds resilience in the learner.

- It can increase determination.

- It develops good sportsmanship.

- It provides a strong environment to self-reflect.

- It can provide added motivation.

- It builds mental strength ('what doesn't break you makes you stronger').

- It enables the learner to develop management of emotional feelings, care and judgement about with whom those feelings are shared.

'Anything to do with horses at any level prepares the rider to manage disappointment and put it in context while at the same time learning to savour the good, successful moments.'

LADY MADELEINE LLOYD WEBBER, President, Pony Club

▶ EQUESTRIAN SCENARIO

Julie had a problem with disappointment. She is very organised and manages the entries, running order, times, clean clothing, etc. for her daughter May, who is a very keen event rider. May loves her riding, training and competing. The whole family enjoy equestrian sport together. Julie's husband drives the lorry and 'grooms' and they support their daughter in every way they can. When things went wrong however, Julie felt out of control and knew she couldn't manage things and make them right; this she found physically gut-wrenching. She knew she should react positively and greet her daughter with a 'positive' first before reflecting on the weaknesses, but she just couldn't help showing the intensity of her disappointment in her face, voice and body language. It got to the stage where May would come out of the arena more concerned with what her mother thought, and looking to see her reaction, rather than being either pleased or disappointed with her own performance. Her first words would be 'What did you think?' Julie's problem was increasingly causing friction between the three of them, but in particular between Julie and her husband. He felt she should be more adult about the disappointment and pull herself together. Julie could not seem to convey to him the awful sick feeling that she had in the pit of her stomach. She did feel bad about her reaction – after all it was only a poor performance, not some sort of disaster that had befallen them. She was, however, building herself up with expectation and then felt this huge disappointment when the result was not what they had hoped for, given how well she knew they had all prepared.

The best thing Julie did was to speak to her daughter's coach. The coach was able to give an impartial and reasoned view without being so emotionally involved. She was close enough to know how passionate and competitive the family were but, as the daughter's coach, was able to see the situation from a different perspective. Initially, Julie felt rather embarrassed to discuss what she felt was an unreasonable reaction to May's performance – after all, she always tried her best. Julie was not proud of how she was unable to deal with her disappointment and found it an extremely difficult thing to air. She perceived it as a serious weakness on her part. She should have been able to support her daughter as her mother, not make her feel worse about what had not gone to plan. The rider's coach made Julie realise that it was a natural feeling and she should not punish herself. The following strategies were established to manage the situation:

- When May underperforms, Julie lets her father make the first point of contact with her when she leaves the arena.

- Julie has discussed with her daughter how she feels, but that it is not her fault and it is only because she so desperately wants her to be successful every time out.

- Julie has told her daughter that she will not ask her 'how it went' but listen to her daughter's opinion, before giving her own. She will then pick one of the positive things May said and reinforce that, before they discuss the 'wish I'd done that's'.

- They all now discuss the performance on the way home and all tell each other how they feel.

- Everyone recognises that they all feel slightly differently about it all.

- The rider wants first to win, and secondly make her parents proud.

- The husband wants first his daughter to win and secondly wants Julie to feel happy too.

- Julie just wants her daughter to win and not have to ever suffer disappointment. She knows this is totally unrealistic and will not prepare her for life, so Julie is adjusting to help them both deal with the disappointments that will inevitably arise.

Disappointment leading to blame

Taking responsibility in any situation requires strength of character, resilience and the ability to self-reflect and then clearly identify the areas of weakness and who was responsible for them. When an emotive situation arises, whether in competition or perhaps in an examination/assessment situation, the outcome of the activity will not necessarily be that either expected, or hoped for. At the point of delivery of the result (not winning a competition, or not meeting the required minimum standard to pass an assessment), the first emotion is intense, overwhelming and can create a reaction in the recipient of the result that is irrational and unprepared. If the initial reaction is not controlled or managed (either by the recipient or those present in support) then words may be said that are bitterly regretted at a later stage.

As a coach or learner, the first and safest rule of managing disappointment is to say as little as possible. Even a moment or two, generated by one or two deep breaths, can buy thinking time, so that the first observation is measured and rational. Counting slowly to ten is often an excellent management strategy.

When success is not achieved, the easy option initially is to lay the blame at someone else's door. For riders, the easiest and closest victim is the horse:

'He spooked at the flowers as I went down the centre line, so the rest of my test was affected.' (Horse's fault)

'If the class had been running to time, I would not have been so stressed when I had to ride later than I expected.' (Organiser's fault)

'We arrived late because we got stuck in traffic so I didn't have enough time to work in properly.' (Driver's fault, or that of traffic en route)

Laying blame at anyone else's door immediately provides the opportunity to opt out of taking any responsibility for the outcome. This approach has to be one of the most limiting aspects of any athlete in terms of personal development.

To blame oneself for every situation is equally limiting. The person who permanently apologises for everything they do – often before they have even tried to do it – is equally inhibited by blaming themselves for their inadequacies.

We live in an era where, as highlighted earlier in this chapter in relation to Kubler-Ross's research on the transition curve, it is common practice to find someone else to blame for non-achievement. Accepting and absorbing the disappointment of non-achievement is, however, fundamental to self-reflection, self-drive and further determination to learn from the experience and progress next time.

▶ EQUESTRIAN SCENARIO

Sandra had attended a UKCC Level 2 coaching course, which she had enjoyed, and was coming forward for the final assessment to prove her competence and achieve certification. She is a mature coach with several years of experience teaching many group sessions in a riding school. Her coaching during the course training has shown competence, but also a tendency to revert to 'telling her riders what to do', especially when she feels under pressure. The UKCC

Level 2 assessment requires that the candidate can demonstrate a range of delivery skills (tell and show pupils, set up an exercise and stand back to allow it to work, question riders and empower them to show independence in what they have been taught). In her Level 2 assessment, Sandra fell into the trap of assuming that her pupils would be quite competent and independent as riders. She assumed their ability, rather than assessing them and finding out that both riders in the group were quite insecure, not very coordinated, and that basics such as working on the correct diagonal in trot were barely established. Sandra tackled the session with determination to show how competent she was. Throughout the session, in her efforts to 'teach the riders lots, showing them how good she was', she failed to notice that they were easily getting tired by being worked quite hard. As they became more tired, the faults increased. The riders found difficulty in maintaining the horses in the gait Sandra wanted. One rider had problems with her trot diagonal and received no basic help to address this fundamental fault. As the session came to a conclusion there was obvious frustration from the coach at the lack of development that she felt she had been able to demonstrate. There was also frustration from the riders as they felt exhausted by the work expected of them, and demoralised that they had obviously not achieved what their coach had expected. Both coach and riders showed clear disappointment in the outcome of the session. In the debrief, Sandra was quick to tell her assessor that the riders were not of a good enough standard for her to be able to demonstrate her good coaching skills in the technical delivery of training. When Sandra did not meet the minimum standard required for competence in Level 2, she submitted a complaint to the governing body running the assessment. Her argument was that the pupils were not good enough and so she was unable to show her competence.

What we can learn from this scenario:

- As a coach, always assess riders and, in discussion with them, agree a plan and a 'lesson goal or aim'.

- Never assume in any situation that a rider has a certain level of competence. They may have, but circumstances on the day can influence whether they can maintain or show that level of ability.

- Observe as you work and constantly liaise with your rider(s) so that confidence is maintained in them and they have some leading input into the direction of the lesson.

- The development of any session must be directed to improving the scales of training of the horse and the improvement of the rider's position and coordination of aids.

- In the above scenario, the riders needed help with position, coordination, effect and application of aids. Coming back to the fundamentals of training both horse and rider is the backbone of any riding coach's delivery.

- The coach fell into the trap of trying to show how competent she was rather than assessing and improving the riders in front of her.

Sandra's appeal to the governing body was not upheld; she must reflect and re-sit the qualification, rather than trying to lay blame elsewhere for her lack of competence.

Reframing

The content of any action, whether by the rider or the coach will, to a degree, be affected by the emotional context that the person brings to the situation. So, a rider who arrives at a competition excited at the prospect of riding well and winning a medal will be free to focus their energy and behaviour on that positive outcome. A rider who arrives slightly depressed about the prospect of not doing well will find it harder to focus their energy and behaviour in a way which will lead to a positive outcome. Emotions can diminish as well as enhance performance. The coach can help the rider reframe their view of what is going to happen to reap the benefits of a positive approach to the situation they are facing.

The coach helps the rider by pointing out to them and reminding them that their emotional context is real, valid and something that they can control. Giving the rider the sense that they are in charge of their emotions, rather than the other way round, can be liberating.

Reframing problem to opportunity

As an individual thinks about, prepares for and engages in something new, there can be a tendency to be concerned with what might go wrong, with difficulties that will occur, and a great deal of energy is put into making sure these difficulties are less likely to arise. Looking forward with trepidation is helpful as a navigational tool, in that it helps in planning to overcome obstacles. However, if the coach can then reframe the problems as opportunities, then the situation is imbued with a positive emotional perspective, that enables energy to be channelled into the aim of attaining higher goals, rather than just diverted around avoiding mistakes. In this way, the coach can change thinking – and therefore feeling – by turning potential problems to potential opportunities. For example, a coach can help a rider to stop worrying about how to get more than a 5 for a test element and focus instead on how to get a 7, and the consequent positive feelings that this would engender. Or a coach can reframe time for an event rider, away from being an enemy, a scarce resource that needs to be beaten, to a friend that gives you a framework to complete the course exactly on time.

In summary, the coach asks the learner to talk through each element of an upcoming situation, getting them to be aware of every time their language indicates a problem and helping them reframe that as an opportunity to transform or transcend the particular problem.

Reframing intensity

Coaches often come across learners whose level of ambition is incremental: to get things right to achieve the next step, to be better than they were yesterday. This is both useful and insufficient. The key lies in reframing next steps into the transformation, doing well into being excellent, being skilful into mastery, turning from being an expert into being an artist, from doing a great round into providing a great sporting moment. When the coach and learner reframe in this way then skill is improved and potential is unleashed.

Reframing through guided visualisation

This technique can be used by coach and learner to carry out detailed planning and execution of a situation as if they were in the situation itself. For example, the equestrian coach and rider work through a guided visualisation of every element of the situation they are facing – each jump, each element of the test, each section of the course. At each crucial point the coach asks the rider what they are thinking and feeling at this particular juncture, taking care to notice negative or less positive thoughts and feelings and then asking the rider to repeat the ride again with a transformational mindset. This can be done/rehearsed many times until the optimum is reached and the new mindset is firmly in place.

Reframing through language

Underlying reframing is the concept of language leading the outcome. If an individual's self-talk – the voice in their head – is negative, mediocre, incremental, then a diminished performance will follow. The same is true with externalised language both between humans and between humans and horses, whether verbal or non-verbal. One of the roles of the coach is to ensure that every conversation returns to the upbeat so that, no matter how daunting the prospect, the learner has anchored within them the absolute prospect of success. The coach can help reframe the learner's general conversation to be positive and make sure they have the thoughts, feelings and language to access the positive in times of high stress.

Reframing through story-telling

Helping the learner reframe their thoughts and feelings by sharing, through story-telling, how the coach has, in their past, maximised potential, overcome adversity and achieved against the odds, can be highly motivational. Learners need the sense that there are examples of others breaking through similar thresholds or barriers that they are facing. Parables, stories with lessons and learning in them, can illuminate possibilities that are difficult to grasp when stressed, disappointed or under- or overwhelmed. The coach can also direct their learners to glean from others how they have reframed their possibilities to be the very best they can be.

Managing success

This must be the easy bit! One would certainly think so, but winning does not come without its share of pitfalls. As coach or learner, successes should be enjoyed, nurtured and valued. Successes are also situations to learn from, if only so that the circumstance of 'leading the pack' can be processed, retained and hopefully reproduced on many future occasions.

Winning generates all the positive feelings of well-being and satisfaction from the competitor, the coach and all the support team who have assisted, sometimes behind the scenes, to contribute to the athlete's ability to win. These moments must all be 'lived and enjoyed'. Of course, they may be repeated and everyone involved hopes they will, but a particular success may also be a one-off occasion and therefore it should be savoured and appreciated, not wasted. There must be countless athletes in a myriad of different sports who only won one Olympic gold medal. That pinnacle of achievement must not be lost in a haze of publicity and frenzy of the moment, quickly passing and not really appreciated at the time. There is only that moment, that time, to celebrate that achievement. If you are there as an athlete, coach or significant other, make sure that the celebration takes place.

After a huge achievement there is inevitably a period of let-down. In equestrian sport the horse, having been carefully prepared for that golden goal, usually has some 'down time'. The horse will be oblivious to the press interest around the win, the aftermath of the rider becoming, for a while, the face of success. The rider then has to learn to live with their newly achieved status. This can be difficult, especially for younger people, who may find that their relationship with other members of their peer group has subtly changed. Once someone climbs to the top of any level of competence, they are there to be challenged; others will want their crown. Some of those opponents will be positive and supportive of the status the victor holds; others will be quietly jealous and envious and a few, sadly, may be openly antagonistic. The successful competitor may find that there are subtle changes in their relationships with others they regarded as equals. People who were open and friendly when this person was 'one of them' begin to avoid having to meet or converse with them, and there can be an unpleasant undercurrent of remarks: 'She was lucky in the draw', 'The judges on that day really like her horse', 'She thinks she's such a great rider but who wouldn't be on that horse?'

Being at the top can be lonely, and the successful competitor might begin to wonder if it was worth it. If those feelings creep in, they should just remember the prize-giving, which they have stored as one of the memories of a lifetime, to be drawn upon whenever life is throwing them a hard time.

Resilience

In sport, developing this quality is probably an essential prerequisite of success. In discussing achievement of successes, and failures, there is an underlying expectation that the coach and learner develop greater resilience as a result of the experience of training and competition. Resilience involves a flexibility and adaptability of the individual to be able to process the information obtained through training or competition, reflect and analyse this constructively and then move forward with greater resolve to improve. Resilience is generally thought to mean springing back, resuming the original shape after bending and readily and quickly recovering from shock. Rather than consider this as 'bouncing back from a setback', why not think of it as bouncing forward with renewed resolve, purpose and vigour, hopefully and probably, reaching a point further on than the point at which the setback occurred. With reference back to Judy Murray's statement in Chapter 2 that 'every setback made him stronger' the athlete and coach in partnership can develop an increased spirit, toughness and purpose to attain the planned goal.

BOUNCING FORWARD

This enthusiasm and confidence are often generated from the athlete's early exposure to sport, whether through family or peer group introduction. A history of commitment and a strong work ethic through upbringing ensures an ongoing pleasure and enjoyment derived from the process of training, as well as the thrill of competition. There must be deep satisfaction achieved through training (see **intrinsic motivation**, page 48), otherwise resilience will be challenged with every setback. In all sports, however, there are examples of athletes coming from families where there is no previous experience or commitment to a specific sport. In some equestrian families there are also examples of one member following a completely different path from the rest of the family, who are nevertheless all on the 'equestrian treadmill' – a good example being the Skeltons, with father Nick a world-class showjumper, and brothers Dan and Harry highly successful in the roles of racehorse trainer and jockey, respectively.

We are at our most resilient when we control the balance of attention we give to the circumstances we are in. We display qualities that create the optimum likelihood for recovery and creativity. There will be a sweet-spot in the range of possible positions on a spectrum that will show and promote resilience. Some of the spectra are:

- Logical/emotional – the coach asks the learner to think through situations in an ordered and rational fashion.

- Determined/flexible – the learner is encouraged not to accept a negative outcome, or that circumstances can't be changed.

- Optimistic/pessimistic – the coach suggests that the learner thinks of what's good.

- Calm/excited – the learner learns not to become easily excited and/or has ways of quickly calming their initial reactions.

The following states in the learner will also help:

- They are rested – a good night's sleep helps clear thinking.

- They are aware of what's going on, so are not taken by surprise.

- They are fit and healthy – this gives the energy to tackle difficult issues.

- They are connected to people from whom they can receive support willingly.

- They are motivated to overcome challenging issues.

Burnout

Unfortunately, there can be very serious consequences for the learner, such as burnout, if their personal blocks take over; if emotional resilience is not increased; if anxiety is not decreased and/or managed. There are three levels of burnout:

1. Emotional exhaustion.

2. Irritation leading to the withdrawal from situations.

3. Shut down.

While the coach must play an important role in noticing any signs of burnout, they may not be equipped to deal with the learner's emotional state. However, as a minimum, they have a responsibility to recommend places/people from where the learner could get the help they need, for example, the involvement of a sport psychologist.

INSIGHTS

- The whole orientation of equestrian competition must be towards achieving the maximum performance from the partnership of horse and rider at the specific time when it matters most.

- Significant others can help or hinder that process and it is important that, gradually, there is an assessment of the part played by any significant others in the rider's development.

- Repressing negative feelings takes energy, therefore, less energy will be available for creative thought.

- The coach should know their learners well enough to step in and support them before stress becomes damaging.

- It is important to recognise and seize opportunities emerging from set-backs, and to tackle difficult situations face-on, rather than avoiding them.

- Success and failure build resilience and mental toughness. As either coach or learner, we need bucket-loads of these characteristics, and work in the equestrian world constantly provides opportunities to build them more and more.

- It is the coach's responsibility to keep the learner psychologically safe when they are going through the transition curve.

- Resilience can be strengthened and developed by good role models, supportive coaching and a clear strategy of development which is constantly flexible and adaptable to the circumstances that arise through training and competition.

5. SPIRITUAL

POINT OF VIEW

As coaches and riders, it is fundamental to be aware and not to forget that the horse lives 'in the moment'. If we indulge in our personal thoughts and worries, we detach ourselves mentally and sometimes physically from the horse. That can create a situation where the horse is lacking leadership and information; he then has to set his own agenda, and harmony in the relationship between horse and rider is compromised. Coaches and riders need to be sensitive and empathetic to others' needs, including those of the horse.

There have been numerous references to the horse during this book and this chapter aims to further explore that unique relationship in equestrian sport. We could and should gain so much knowledge and expertise by studying other sports. There is no avoiding the fact, however, that equestrian sport involves another living, breathing, thinking, feeling creature. The horse was not put on this planet to become an Olympic athlete; he becomes involved in a partnership with his rider through no choice of his own.

'Being coached gives you the help you need to fully understand your horse and his behaviour.'

SCOTT BRASH MBE,
Olympic gold medallist,
Team GBR showjumping

This chapter will therefore look more deeply and sympathetically into the 'spiritual' communication between horse and rider and consider how much of that is innate and how much can be learnt, developed and strengthened by both coach and rider.

THE RELATIONSHIP BETWEEN THE HORSE AND RIDER

Awareness of the unique relationship

This is what sets equestrian sport apart from all other sports. If you are aiming to be a top golfer or a top tennis player, after the need to beat the individual above you in the current sport ranking, another concern is where to store your inanimate piece of equipment! That equipment may be the best that money can buy, but it is still inanimate and its reaction is entirely and literally in the player's hands. Not so the horse. The horse has a definite mind of his own. There arises a vital partnership between horse and rider and then a three-way relationship that involves the coach. It is the strength of that relationship that can dictate the success of the partnership between horse and rider. The FEI (Fédération Equestre Internationale), the international governing body of equestrian sport, has as its philosophy that the horse in sport must be a 'happy athlete'. We, as riders and coaches, must have that philosophy at the heart of our endeavours to achieve at any level with our horses. The horse must be a willing partner, as he has no choice; he has no way other than in his behaviour to show his disinclination. We have a moral responsibility to train the horse to the best of our ability and constantly assess his competence, confidence, understanding and enthusiasm to carry out what we hope and expect of him.

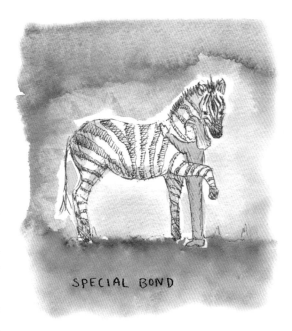

SPECIAL BOND

Riders have goals, which will hopefully be structured, planned, realistic and achievable. The horse is never party to these goals. His goal is to put his head down and eat grass, preferably with other horses, to run away if he is frightened and, if this is not possible, then to fight. If he has to, he will bite, kick, or buck to offload something on his back that terrifies him. To establish a positive relationship with the horse we must have a fundamental empathy, an understanding of him, compassion for his role in our life, and sympathy for his commitment to a goal he has not, in any way, been involved in establishing. We must be able to and interested in recognising the well-being of our horses, for example:

- How healthy he is.

- How fit he is.

- How able he is to fulfil the work regime to which we are subjecting him.

- How he reacts when working in terms of confidence, willingness and generosity, which indicates enthusiasm for and understanding of the work.

- In other words, whether he is a 'happy athlete'.

Within our sport there are countless opportunities to learn from experience, as discussed in Chapter 2. Throughout these experiences and when gaining an understanding of the horse's instinctive reactions, we forget at our peril that the horse is unpredictable, reactionary if frightened and then dangerous, owing to his size and weight, when he resorts to instinctive behaviour. As a coach you will hear, on many occasions, the following statement: 'He's never done that before' – usually from less experienced riders or their significant others.

From the following three examples of incidents that elicited the above comment, we can draw some conclusions that may help us in our relationship with the horse.

▶ EQUESTRIAN SCENARIO 1

A rider was working in at a regional championships and there was a small fenced-off area for riders to stand safely to have their horses' boots/bandages removed. This rider was next to go and moved to the enclosed area. The rider's mother, with no warning *whatsoever,* moved directly to the horse's hind leg and started to unstrap one hind boot. The horse was completely taken by surprise and, on feeling something 'attacking' his hind leg, he plunged onto his forelegs and gave a mighty 'double-barrelled' kick out with both hind legs. The unfortunate lady was caught with both hind feet directly into her stomach and was thrown backwards with a force that laid her out flat on her back. The outcome was an air ambulance to hospital – fortunately no lasting damage was done.

▶ EQUESTRIAN SCENARIO 2

A rider was schooling on a warm day and, after a while, became hot and stopped abruptly with no warning. She dropped the reins on the horse's neck and started to take off her blouson jacket. When both her arms where behind her back and she was in a position where both arms were rendered useless to regain the reins, there was a sudden commotion and the horse was unexpectedly startled. He rushed forward and the rider was unbalanced and jerked backwards. Feeling the unsteadiness of his rider, the horse reacted further in fright, putting his head between his knees and plunging. The rider, struggling to get out of her jacket, fell off to the side and backwards and was lucky not to get kicked as well. She was bruised and badly shaken, but was fortunate not to sustain any lasting damage.

▶EQUESTRIAN SCENARIO 3

A rider was working in for a competition with many other horses. All seemed calm and the rider stopped to have her tack checked before being ready to compete. As she moved off again, the horse suddenly, and for no apparent reason, buried his head between his knees, bucked and twisted, almost unseating the rider. The rider stayed on but the horse continued to buck and twist. The rider managed to dismount and attempted to calm the horse. With help, the rider took the horse out of the working-in area and, as he settled, she removed the saddle, making a thorough check to ensure that there was nothing pinching or uncomfortable. Nothing was found and the tack was replaced. The horse was still very tense and the rider understandably anxious. With help and support the rider tentatively remounted the horse and was led around for two circuits. Her time to enter the arena was fast approaching and the rider trotted and cantered cautiously around for the last time and entered the arena. The horse took a deep breath and the rider felt this and was able to get him 'with her'. The test was fluent and harmonious and the partnership won the class on a good score, 3 per cent ahead of the competition.

What can we learn from these scenarios?

Scenarios 1 and 2. The horse in each situation was taken completely by surprise and both victims (those injured) took the horse for granted. In both cases, when frightened, the horse instantly reverted to instinctive behaviour to protect himself. Both incidents were results of the assumption that the horse would behave predictably in all situations.

Scenario 3. 'Something' upset the horse (probably, the rider will never know what). In that unexpected case, everything that could be done was done, to bring the horse back to confident, calm behaviour and the rider was brave and positive enough to restore the horse's confidence in her. Significant others at the scene also reacted in a constructive, helpful way to reinstate 'normal' behaviour.

The learning from all these scenarios is: never take any horse for granted, always maintain awareness and ensure that you 'inform' the horse of everything that you may 'do to him'. However well you know him, he has the potential to hurt you and himself, through no fault of his own.

In short, we must care about our horse and know when he is 'happy'. This comes from years of loving horses, looking after horses and developing 'horsemanship', not only from using them as a commodity for earning money or winning medals. Horses thrive in an environment where there is consistency in management and training. Regular regimes of feeding, handling and training will ensure good health and mental well-being. Recognition of the horse as a herd animal, a simple thinker who enjoys other equine company and time to 'be a horse' is essential. In return, the horse develops trust and confidence in his human 'partner'; he is loyal and hard-working and will give his utmost in a sharing partnership of understanding, compassion and leadership.

Understanding different brain reactions

The challenge that a coach of equestrian athletes has always to consider and address is the balance between improving the horse (training the equine athlete) and improving the rider. The horse is quite a simple thinker. He eats to survive, he runs away, kicks, bites, bucks or rears to survive and he likes to be in a group as he is instinctively a herd animal. As such he is a 'follower' not a leader; he is fundamentally non-aggressive, as he is prey rather than predator.

The rider, on the other hand, has a very complex brain. That brain has all the survival mechanisms of the horse. Fear for example, will generate an intense rush of adrenalin and instinctively create 'flight mode' or 'fight mode'; these feelings can be identified immediately before competing or before tackling a challenge that is not entirely familiar. However, the human brain has an enhanced ability to process information, rationalise and balance arguments for or against an action. This can enable management of the instinctive 'flight and/or fight mode' and, in fact, turn it into an advantage of 'heightened awareness' to improve competition performance. In addition to this rational brain, there are times when the human brain is very irrational! The irrational brain is very strong and sometimes takes control when least expected. It is a human survival mechanism, but an awareness of it is essential – live with it, as there is no opportunity to get rid of it. Good management of the irrational brain is a huge asset to the competitor! Poor management of the irrational brain can, however, be destructive. For example, the rational brain may be saying that the rider can win, everything has been put in place to ensure success, but the irrational brain may be throwing in the 'what ifs?' – 'What if the horse goes lame?', 'What if the judge who doesn't like me is there? Doubts, temptations and perceived crises are all products of the irrational brain. The more the rider can 'think in the moment' to manage current circumstances, the more they will be in tune with the way the horse thinks, and that will produce harmony.

BRAIN REACTIONS

The horse does not have that irrationality; he reacts only to the way he has been trained, or to the experiences that he has had, that have caused him to be confident or fearful. The horse expects to and relies on having leadership to guide him. The rider is the 'leader' of his herd and he gains confidence in that leadership, he then flourishes under that leadership and enters wholeheartedly into a bold and confident partnership with his rider.

▶ EQUESTRIAN SCENARIO

Hugh is a middle-aged workaholic. He runs his own business and is extremely successful in every respect. When he wants to achieve something, he is in a position financially and with huge innate drive and commitment, to 'make it happen'. What Hugh wants, Hugh almost always gets. He is well-educated, hard-working and unmarried so has little restriction, if any, on his large available disposable income. As a child Hugh rode actively and successfully in the Pony Club and thoroughly enjoyed Pony Club eventing until his career and adult life got in the way. Hugh has not ridden for around twenty years, but he has remained fit by maintaining a regime of going to the gym, playing tennis and swimming within his hectic business life. Hugh decides that it's time he returned to his passion of riding and has great aspirations to event competitively. He has fence-judged a few times at local BE competitions and is fired up by the obvious adrenalin rush he sees achieved by the cross-country ride. Hugh knows a good livery yard close to where he lives; the owner Fran was in the Pony Club with Hugh and chose to go into the horse industry as a profession. She has worked hard to develop an excellent reputation as a rider and coach and frequently has good young event horses for sale, which she has produced. Within a few months Hugh has bought himself a six-year-old Thoroughbred horse that has completed three Novice events with double clear rounds (showjumping and cross-country) and secure dressage scores; in fact the horse has won once and been well placed on the other occasions. The horse has been written up in *Horse & Hound* as being a horse to watch for the future, as he has a big, bold jump and nothing has bothered him across country. All the horse's education to date has been with Fran, who has produced many similar good young horses that go on to consistent success.

Over the next few months Hugh aims to develop a competitive partnership with the horse. Despite having hardly ridden over the past twenty years, he has often said: 'It's like riding a bike – you never forget how!' He has a number of lessons with Fran who advises that he does not rush into competing with the horse. Fran continues to school the horse when Hugh has no time to ride. Hugh finds time to do the fast work but leaves the dressage to Fran. He makes frequent excuses that he hasn't got time to do the 'boring stuff' and 'that's your job'. After about six weeks he takes the horse to a BE90, although Fran has suggested a couple of cross-country schooling sessions and some unaffiliated showjumping as a preparation. Hugh intended to do as Fran advised but 'never has time'. Fran has also advised caution in starting BE eventing too soon; as she feels a season of consolidating the separate disciplines of an event would benefit Hugh and the horse greatly. Hugh ignores this advice and is anxious to get going. The first event is less than successful; the dressage test is tense and stressful for horse and rider. The showjumping is hectic, with three fences down, and the cross-country is fast and increasingly lacking harmony and control. In debrief after the event, Hugh tells Fran that the horse was a lunatic, he felt out of control and he needs to have a stronger bit. He suggests she needs to 'sort out' the dressage and, since he will be away on business next week, could she ride the horse all week and improve things for when he next comes to ride. Fran's input and feedback on the situation is, in general, ignored by Hugh. His opinion is that the horse is trained, he will soon get back into the swing of things 'he is just a bit lacking practice' and next time will be fine.

Having read this scenario you may consider that it is unrealistic and not true to life. If only that were the case! All the scenarios in this book are genuine cases – only the names have been changed. Let's give some consideration to the many issues this example highlights:

The horse

- Is a promising and able young horse that has been trained by a professional rider through his early development. That rider is probably lighter in weight than the new owner, certainly of a completely different level of competence, and is a full-time horsewoman.

- Some have the opinion that female riders establish a different empathy/feeling with the horse from male riders. This opinion needs to be considered if a man is taking over a horse that has been produced by a woman and vice versa.

- In this scenario Fran is a professional rider, has trained this horse over a period of many months, and Hugh is an amateur rider who has many other major priorities in his life. His horse represents the recreational and fun aspect of life, on which he does not want to have to focus too much effort and concentration. He just wants to enjoy himself and win. He judges success against how many times he wins.

- The horse, having had absolute consistency in his training and competitions to date is, within a short time, introduced to a different rider in terms of size, weight, ability, expectations and empathy and subjected to competition with a rider who is far less knowledgeable, but has far higher goals and expectations of the horse than his original rider.

- In competition, the horse is lacking the leadership and security that he obtained from his original partner and so reacts in the way that is instinctive to him when he is frightened or confused. He 'runs away'.

The rider

- His recent experience is limited and his expectation is high.

- Hugh can afford a 'good horse' and he wants to achieve – in this case win – as he does in every other aspect of his life.

- His commitment to the goal is unrealistic in relation to the complexity of the 'goal'. Hugh has no commitment to the structure or process of achieving the goal. In fact he has no awareness of a need to be involved in the goal! His *only* goal is to be successful and he believes he has invested considerable funds in a horse that will realise that goal, and that is his right.

- His belief is, that with a horse that has ability and a past record of competence, his own courage and tenacity will be sufficient to overcome any shortcomings that may result from lack of recent experience.

- He chooses to ignore the complexity of the sport he 'played at' as a child and convinces himself that, on a good horse, he is good enough to move back into a sport that he enjoyed in the past.

This relationship is doomed to failure. Within the evolving situation, the horse will suffer through no fault of his own. Hugh and Fran will also suffer, as they struggle to realise their diverse aims and manage the inevitable frustrations that lack of achievement will arouse. The only way that the relationship between horse, rider and coach will have any chance of a future, is if Hugh radically changes his outlook and mindset on the whole situation. Fran has a challenge on her hands. Hugh will only begin to do this if, through discussion on both sides, and reasonable planning, goal-setting and feedback, Hugh begins to believe in and sign up to a realistic plan of progress for him and his horse; a plan that will hopefully begin to realise small goals that will motivate Hugh to aim for more. The horse is the innocent party in all of this; he will continue to react directly to the situations he finds himself in day by day as he 'lives in the moment'.

Therefore, the coach and rider would need to resolve the following issues:

- The rider has a genuine and currently misinformed understanding of the current level of the sport of eventing.

- The twenty years since Hugh was in Pony Club have seen an evolution of a highly competitive sport where the levels of each of the three 'disciplines' – dressage, showjumping and cross-country are now structured, sophisticated and require a high level of competence if the rider is to be competitive.

- A commitment to that level of competence would require Hugh to share with Fran an honest plan of his current strengths (e.g. tenacity, determination, financial viability, enthusiasm) against his weaknesses (lack of time, inconsistency of riding/training, and commitment to the effort involved in developing skill and improvement), that will ensure better chance of success.

Until a structure is in place to address these issues, the poor horse will remain in a state of disruption. He has moved from the complete consistency that he has had throughout his young life, to being thrown into a situation where sometimes he has that consistency when Fran rides him and sometimes he is like a 'rudderless ship'; he has no guidance, no consistency and is having to manage a completely different situation when Hugh rides him. The horse may end up the ultimate casualty of this situation. Several unsuccessful outings and one or two vociferous accounts of the horse's inconsistent performance from Hugh may taint the horse with a reputation he does not deserve.

> 'Coaching is all about developing physical and mental harmony, suppleness and cooperation. The result is not how well the horse or rider performs, but how well they work together.'
>
> **JOHN LEDINGHAM,** Irish international showjumping rider and coach

In every sport other than equestrian sport, to progress up the levels you must beat the person ranking above you. That commitment to skill and achievement is fundamental in all other sport. In equestrian sport this is not the case. It is possible for a rider to achieve above their level of skill, knowledge and competence if they are mounted on a talented or experienced horse. This should not be a reason for underestimating the commitment and ability of a rider and should also not be a reason for having a lack of high regard for a rider who has access through funds or background to the best horses and training that money can buy. Some success will inevitably come to riders who are in the fortunate position where they can 'learn their trade' on the best horses available. There is a value in the saying that 'good horses make good riders'. However, in order to ultimately achieve the highest level of competence, those riders *will* have to learn the skill of bringing out the best in their horse.

> 'I was buying a horse from friends and Ulrik told me: "Less is more" (the horse was of a higher calibre than I'd ridden before). I've been able to carry that through with every other horse. It's all about partnership, and small subtle aids can make a big difference, especially in para (given our disabilities) where if things can be easier – it can really help.'
>
> **NATASHA BAKER MBE,** Olympic Para rider and gold medallist

TRAINING HORSE AND RIDER

While we stated earlier that the remit of this book is not about training the horse or rider, but about educating coaches and learners, it would be a missed opportunity not to make some reference to the basic system of educating horse and rider. We have talked extensively about the partnership between horse and rider and discussed the relationship between them. Confidence and harmony are key, as are communication and feel. There has been reference to the horse needing to understand the 'new communication aids' from a change of rider and the confusion caused when the new information is unclear or inconsistent. We have talked much about harmony and partnership, sometimes relating to the coach-learner relationship, but always at the heart of equestrian coaching is the horse-rider partnership. Some coaches are great trainers of horses and some coaches teach the rider good technique, but sometimes at the horse's expense. The greatest coaches are those who can balance the need for educating the horse effectively and on secure training lines, while developing the core stability, balance, effectiveness and coordination of the rider. Harmony and feel are fundamental in the partnership between these two living 'creatures'.

Riding is a sport and although the horse 'carries' the rider, the rider must have a commitment to their own fitness, suppleness and physical development so that they enhance the horse's natural ability, whether that is to gallop, jump or carry out athletic, gymnastic movements. The rider must never be an encumbrance to the horse. The partnership between horse and rider should be one of seamless communication and power.

A progressive system

For many decades, Germany has had a historically strong system of breeding and training competition horses, and has been one of the most successful nations in all the Olympic equestrian disciplines. Their training system has, in recent years, been embraced worldwide and can be identified under the well-recognised 'Scales of Training'.

All coaches of riders, in whatever discipline, will aim to develop the horse's training and the rider's effectiveness and skill. We have discussed the horse's welfare as being paramount in our role as either coach or rider; his confidence and understanding of what we are asking of him as being essential. By adhering to the Scales of Training we can ensure a smooth progression of the horse's training, following a system that is proven.

Relaxation is the key to a confident equine performer. Relaxation comes from the stability and consistency of the rider, and also from the confidence of the environment in which the horse is kept, his lifestyle and his management. Relaxation then gives the foundation for the Scales of Training to be developed through addressing the following criteria:

Rhythm: In all three gaits. Rhythm = Regularity. Linked to rhythm is tempo, or speed of the rhythm, and the beginning of balance.

Suppleness: The developing elasticity within the horse's body which enables him to work evenly on both reins and become responsive to turns, circles and lateral work.

Contact/connection: The elastic connection that is established between the active pushing power of the hind legs, over a supple back, into the submissive acceptance to the rider's hand, with the poll as the highest point.

Impulsion: This is contained energy; the horse reacts actively to the rider's leg and the energy is contained in the submissive acceptance of the hands, thus there is supple vibrancy in the horse's whole body between leg and hand.

Straightness: With rhythm, suppleness and contact in evidence, it is possible to make the horse straight in his body and even in the reins. The development of more balance, by actively engaged hind legs and increasing self-carriage, allows for more cadence and suspension in the trot and canter.

Collection: The horse is able to take more weight onto his hind legs and therefore lighten the forehand and 'carry himself'. He can open and close his frame while maintaining energy and balance for ease of movement. He seeks a steady contact but maintains self-carriage without a dependency on the rider's hand for any support.

Rider's seat and aids

While developing the horse's education through the Scales of Training, the rider should be constantly seeking to achieve an independent seat which is in complete balance with the horse in all gaits. Harmony can then be achieved by subtle and coordinated light aids, which are imperceptible to the observer. The rider's position and balance on the horse becomes the most effective 'tool' for the rider's communication and interaction with the horse. Neglect of this area of development may contribute to weakness in the even effect of the rider's aids and subsequent unlevel physical development of the horse or rider. The inevitable outcome will be a horse and rider who put themselves at risk of injury or physical weaknesses as a result of uneven pressures on parts of the body. It is beyond the scope of this book to discuss in depth the methods of rider development. Suffice to say, it is a fundamental 'building block' in the enhanced development of horse and rider as a compatible, athletic partnership. The rider should commit fully to becoming as good an athlete as possible themselves, as they strive to make their horse a top equine performer.

Managing feelings and learning 'feel'

With this wonderful animal that we invite to be our 'partner in sport', we need to consider his 'intelligence'. It is very small in terms of reasoning power and decision-making, in comparison to ours. He learns through repetition and that puts a huge responsibility on us as riders and trainers, to ensure that the lessons he learns are clear, repeated consistently and rewarded in the same way, when carried out in response to that clear information. The horse does not understand human emotions; he has no idea about juvenile tantrums, teenage frustrations, midlife crises or adult irritations, such as not having time to ride before picking the kids up from school. The horse, however, often has to deal with the reactions on him of those human emotions and he has no innate mechanism to do that.

Let's give more thought to the management of the relationship between the horse, who has little if any mechanism for dealing with other's emotions, and the rider, who may be highly emotionally charged and show random and unpredictable mood-swings. The rider's emotions are also likely to be heightened during competition. To ensure a secure and reliable partnership, the rider must learn to manage their emotions and not let them affect or disturb the relationship with the horse.

We live in an age of instant gratification. We send a text or email and expect an instant reply. Methods of communication have never been more diverse or more versatile, but sometimes in this 'instant world' we forget at our peril that the horse is still a horse, very similar to how he was millennia ago. We expect him to do canter pirouettes for a mark of 10, jump 1.60m with ease and gallop around a lengthy and demanding cross-country course faultless and without time faults. If we removed the tack from this equine athlete, he would not practise his dressage and jumping for a moment; he would revert to what he wants to do – go and eat grass!

Juvenile riders often vent their frustration on their horse: 'Why does he behave like this, he was perfect yesterday, why does he have to be so awful today?' 'He was perfect while I was working in and then when I entered the arena it all changed.' The answer to that is always 'The horse is a horse; he didn't plan to be difficult today.' It is always the rider's management on the day, that either enables an optimum performance, or contributes to a less satisfactory one.

The coach and rider should have a shared responsibility to crave and seek to achieve as good a relationship with the horse they are training as they can. This means that there must be a desire to understand the horse: how he thinks, what makes him behave the way he sometimes does and how they can best manage this in their training. As with the rider, the horse will demonstrate behaviour linked to past experiences. Sometimes these experiences will not be immediately evident in the picture. A horse bred or purchased as a foal by the trainer, will have a background entirely known to the trainer, whereas a horse bought as an eight-year-old will have eight previous years of 'history', which may be completely hidden to the new owner. Finding out the past history of a horse can be a rocky road and is beyond the remit of this book. Suffice to say that the more background one can glean about a horse

A UNIQUE EQUINE

when a purchase is made, the easier it can be to understand behavioural shortcomings that arise during the establishment of the new partnership.

In the twenty-first century we are constantly aware of 'feelings'. 'How did you feel?' is the question frequently asked first immediately after a success, a crisis or a disaster. Let's consider within sport how often we see a top athlete accosted after winning or losing some competition to explain 'how they felt'. Feelings are about sentiment, emotion, and mood. So where does the horse come in on all that? Feelings are also about 'reaction' and 'sensitivity'. In training the equine athlete, we are aiming for instant and consistent reaction and sensitivity; we strive for 'mental harmony, suppleness and cooperation' (as expressed in John Ledingham's quote on page 131). If you refer back to the text about Hugh's horse earlier this chapter (pages 127–131), it will be evident that he would be receiving inconsistent messages depending on whether he was ridden by Fran or Hugh. How, in these circumstances, can the horse's performance hope to be consistent?

The coach's role is therefore multi-faceted, in recognising the horse's response to the information he is receiving from the rider, and then managing the rider, to interpret and work with these responses to develop performance of the partnership.

'Feel' can be taught through the following means:

- Video observation and relating what the rider sees to what is happening at that moment, and what they then can discern through that moment.

- Riding different horses through a similar pattern of movement and identifying the differences in 'feel' of each horse.

- Riding horses of varying sensitivity to gain a different awareness of that reaction.

- Riding a trained horse that will react accordingly to a series of 'aids' or information, for the rider to develop a 'feel' of those responses. These schoolmasters can develop 'feel' in an unskilled rider.

- Ultimately 'feel' is developed through repetition, visual support from the coach and a great deal of practice.

Although some would debate whether 'feel' in the rider can be taught, if you ask a rider who has suffered a disability they will tell you that a new response *can* be learnt. Of course, if there is physical damage resulting in loss of limb or nerve malfunction then a different pathway of awareness must be established. However, if you watch a blind rider, you will recognise how their awareness of 'feel', in respect of sensitivity to minute differences in their own balance and that of their horse is heightened, because they are not able to use their sight. If you ride for a few seconds with your eyes closed you will immediately experience a far greater awareness of your body movement and sense of balance, both of which you normally manage by using your eyes for alignment.

'Feel' is more innate (sharper, more sensitive, more reactive) in some riders than in others. The same applies to horses. A horse has the sensitivity naturally to feel a fly on any part of his body and, through a tiny ripple of his skin muscles, he can cause it to leave! He also has the sensitivity, partly instinctive, but also learnt through good training, to move from walk to gallop at the start of a race, to move from piaffe to passage, or to jump a fence of 1.60m from a tight corner.

'A clear message creating the foundations of a forward rhythm and straightness from the legs into the hands making it easier for a good eye, while giving confidence.'

DI LAMPARD, Team GBR Showjumping Performance Manager and Coach

The other side of the coin is that a horse can also become inured to heavy, uncoordinated, unknowledgeable aid applications, to the extent that he more or less ignores them.

Developing empathy

We discussed in Chapter 4 the need for emotional resilience in order to learn from and therefore bounce forward after setbacks. Also, in Chapter 2, we highlighted the benefits of self-awareness. Coaches and riders who have developed these skills could be described as having emotional intelligence (EQ). This competence, in many environments, is now recognised as being as important as intellectual ability (IQ), as it results in empathy which, in turn, is essential for building relationships. In fact, in his book *Emotional Intelligence*, Daniel Goleman, the psychologist and co-founder of the Collaborative for Academic, Social and Emotional Learning, argues that EQ matters more than IQ. More specifically, we need to understand our own feelings and recognise emotions in others; and be able to put ourselves in other's shoes.

> 'I sometimes think I have more empathy with horses than with people.'
>
> **SIR ANTHONY McCOY OBE,** multiple national hunt champion jockey over three decades

In addressing the relationship between stress and empathy, Professor David Peters, Clinical Director at the Faculty of Science and Technology, Westminster University's Centre for Resilience, makes a number of points which are reproduced here with his permission:

– If we're functioning in a stressed state (hunted), or chasing goals (hunting), our perspective is narrowed – we therefore won't make good decisions or communicate in an optimum way.

– This is because, when we feel under pressure, the mammalian mid-brain turns off the prefrontal cortex – the newer, cleverer brain. Stress also reduces empathy – we miss the clues as to how others (people and maybe horses too) are feeling.

– We've always known that there's a connection between the brain and the heart, however, it has only been more recently understood that there is far more communication in the other direction – from the heart to the brain.

EMPATHY

– The heart doesn't beat like metronome; its rhythm varies, and it varies less when we are stressed. Good heart rate variability is a sign of good health and vitality, indicating there is flexibility in the 'autonomic' nervous system. This is important because this is the part that controls basic processes in the body, such as blood pressure and digestion. And we all know how negative emotions can raise blood pressure, turn us pale with fear, upset our digestion. Well, it now seems that positive emotions are actually good for the body and good for the brain.

HEART BEAT

– A powerful and immediate way to increase heart rate variability is to regulate our breathing to around 6 breaths in a minute – not deep but slow and steady. Practising this regularly can help the body learn what it feels like to relax and feel a sense of safety, so we are less likely to drop into the flight/fight response. And, when we feel tense or anxious, taking longer outbreaths is useful, as this slows the heart down and helps reduce the body's threat response. Paying attention to taking long, slow out-breaths is an easy way to reduce tension during any activity.

– Most sports psychologists agree that we perform best when we feel calmer, less tense and emotionally positive. The coach should help the rider achieve a relaxed, positively focused state. This is what martial arts masters aim for: a state of mind and body that allows greater awareness, intuition and sensitivity.

– In order to promote this state, the coach could intervene in the following ways:

  • Encourage the rider to see how it feels to practise changing their breathing pattern as outlined above.

  • Ask the rider to practise noticing the way feelings express themselves as tensions in the body.

- Practise feeling positive emotions: appreciation and gratitude for instance produce powerful positive changes in the way the human brain works!

- Check that their own coaching attitude, rather than dwelling on what's wrong, always centres on helping the rider notice 'mindfully' the things that don't serve them well, and to inspire them to experience and appreciate what's good about any situation.

MINDFULNESS

For most of us, this is a learnable skill, although for the person described in the following scenario, this was a huge challenge. Although the following situation happened within a business context, it further illustrates our assertions in this chapter.

▶CORPORATE SCENARIO

Steve was promoted from the Head of IT to Sales Director in a large manufacturing company. He did not want the job but was told that he had to take it. He was comfortable in his previous role where he particularly enjoyed developing project plans and researching new software solutions. Steve's contact with staff and internal clients in the old job was minimal as he was able to delegate these relationship responsibilities to his senior management team. In the main he had a great deal of common ground with his colleagues, and cherished the technical challenge of the role. The IT function had forty employees.

Soon after his promotion, Steve started to struggle. His anxiety, as identified by others – not himself, came to a head whilst planning the forthcoming sales conference. He was informed that he would be faced with 750 very assertive salesmen, whom others had reported as a feisty group who were difficult to influence. There was an expectation based on past conferences that the impending residential event would be highly interactive, with lots of social events over three days. Steve appeared quite daunted about leading this meeting, so an executive coach was suggested. The coach, having heard a factual account of the promotion process, with dates and a description of tasks from Steve, asked the question: 'How do you feel about your current situation?' Steve's answer was: 'I'm sorry, but I don't understand the question.' This response, alongside Steve's general demeanour (rather Mr Spock-like), and how the Chief Executive had described him, led the coach to appreciate the enormity of the 'task'. What followed were a number of intensive discussions with the coach about what was blocking Steve's ability to be aware of his feelings, and many behaviour rehearsals with feedback, practising more personal and empathetic reactions to others.

How horses interact with humans

In recent years there have been two very powerful films – *The Horse Whisperer* and *War Horse* – both were Hollywood blockbusters, adapted from books and based on true stories by their respective authors. These films appealed to the age-old relationship between man and horse, that unidentified emotional link that can become incredibly strong, especially when either party is under duress. Recent research (cited in 'Horses recognise expression', *Horse & Hound* 18 Feb 2016), has proved that horses can tell our emotions by identifying variations in facial expression. This should come as little surprise to those of us who have a lifetime's love of or experience with horses. Even the uninitiated rider will often say 'The horse knew I was scared and that's why he ran away with me.' Fear is visible and tangible and, the more evident it is, the more another being will react to it. As we have discussed previously, horses are followers by nature and require a leader. The rider, as leader, gives the horse confidence to work in partnership with them. As the leadership develops, so do the trust and partnership between horse and rider. Of course the horse will have his own thoughts and feelings about life, but if he was not fundamentally a 'follower' we would have much more difficulty in training him. He is generally a willing and compliant partner as long as the information he is given is:

- Clear.

- Consistent.

- Repetitive.

- Applied in small steps of development.

- Backed up by rewards for his compliance.

As mentioned on pages 123–4, the horse has instinctive reactions, but the more secure and confident he is in his training regime and his environment, the more the instinctive reactions will remain suppressed. Only when the confidence or secure environment is disturbed, will the instinctive reactions escape to the surface and threaten the equilibrium between horse and rider. The wisdom and experience of the more mature coach and rider will be quick to recognise the 'trigger point' that caused the instinctive reactions to overcome the dependable trained horse's reactions.

The late and great Molly Sivewright FBHS was ahead of her time when she wrote the wonderful publications *Thinking Riding* (parts one and two). She wrote extensively about the 'thought aid'. In these days of instant grati-fication, there is too much expectation of the horse 'coming up with the goods'. From the post-war period onward, there has been an increasing emphasis on breeding horses specifically for sporting purposes. In addition to the longer-established quest for more speed in racehorses, there has been great emphasis on quality of movement and athleticism in dressage horses and showjumpers. Despite these developments, the 'absolutes' (in terms of maximum speed, jumping height, etc.) have increased only a little, but the overall standard of competition has gone up because we have moved forward with painstaking progression to train our horses to be more athletic and fitter, and for riders to be more competent and focused.

We also understand our own physical and emotional well-being and development better than ever before, but we are sometimes at risk of attrib-uting human emotions and tendencies to our horses. This happens more with younger riders, who have not yet managed to detach their feelings and emotions from those of their horse. They are often convinced that the horse is 'behaving badly just to be difficult'.

One of the obstacles to overcome in training young people is to encourage them to realise that the horse thinks in a completely different way from how riders think. Once they recognise that the emotions they are feeling and demonstrating will have a positive or negative effect on their horse, then great progress can be made in detaching the emotions of horse and rider.

▶EQUESTRIAN SCENARIO

It is a Tuesday evening in summer and John is taking a group of riders for a Pony Club training session. There is a mixture of boys and girls in a group of five and all have been at school all day and have come to training straight from school. The session progresses satisfactorily, but there is a general lack of concentration from most of the riders. Some of the boys are verging on being unruly and, in general, the progression is limited, as the riders are not always engaged with John.

The next session for this group is a couple of weeks later on a Sunday morning. The group of riders are the same and, on this occasion, John sets an exercise which he considers relevant to the standard of ability the group showed at the last session. This time the riders are all focused and involved, the first exercise is done well and John moves on to a more challenging piece of work. All the riders excel and both coach and riders leave the session with a great sense of satisfaction and achievement.

What a difference the time of day makes: after school, children will often be tired – physically maybe not, but mentally yes. On a Sunday morning with no school on Saturday, the same children will have a different mental application. The physical and mental application of the rider to their riding is of great relevance to the outcome of training. The coach needs to be aware of variations in the rider's emotional state, as it can have an effect on their efficiency in riding their horse.

On the whole, the horse doesn't vary very much. He will vary in physical fitness and in mental application depending on his age and stage of training, but he will not show the emotional variations in behaviour that may be present in the rider.

Thinking time

Thinking time is fundamental in the coach-rider relationship. Many riders are 'activists' (see page 71) – they want to 'get on with it', not 'think about it first'. The nature of our equestrian sport is dependent in many cases on an instant response. The rider believes that, to elicit instant response from their horse, they must be quick in their aid application. However, timing and decisiveness in aid application are so important. That involves *thinking*. The rider must be able to 'get inside the horse's head', think how he is thinking, and then relate the aid application to his ability to respond.

If the coach says to the rider 'Make a transition to canter' and the rider immediately applies the aids to canter with no thought for the state of the horse, the canter transition (if it happens) may lack fluency, harmony and coordination. The coach would be better saying 'In your own time, canter'; they can then observe the thinking and preparation of the rider. If the rider receives the command to make a transition to canter, there should be a realistic delay while the following happens:

- The rider hears the command.

- The rider feels the balance and activity of the horse and thinks about where and how soon the aid to canter may be given.

- The rider adjusts the way of going of the horse if necessary.

- The rider chooses the moment when they believe the best transition can be made, and …

- The aid is then given.

Thinking and preparation time are absolutely essential in every horse-rider partnership. That time may be minimal in an educated rider on a well-trained horse and it shows in an apparently seamless relationship between horse and rider. However, thinking, feeling and preparation time is *always* there; it just might not be visible.

Schoolmasters

There is a misinformed perception that 'buying a schoolmaster' can ensure progression to success with more ease than buying an uneducated horse. A horse or pony that is well established at a level of competence in any discipline in equestrian sport, may command a much higher price than an untrained horse. There are advantages to be gained in putting an inexperienced rider on a trained horse, but there are also wrong assumptions made, and inevitable pitfalls. As indicated in the earlier scenario about Hugh (page 127), the building of a relationship between horse and rider should be a gradual and evolving process and it is dependent on many factors. Take a three-year-old horse with good gaits, good conformation and an athletic, supple natural flexibility. The possibility of such a horse becoming an Olympic horse, in any discipline, is dependent on:

- The skill, knowledge and competence of the rider(s).

- The skill, knowledge and competence of the coach(es).

- The temperament and trainability of the horse.

- The physical well-being and soundness of the horse.

- The working relationship between the rider, the horse and the coach as the facilitator.

- And all the above factors coming together at the right time!

Perhaps it would be easier to win the lottery!

Take the educated horse that has achieved a high level of success with one rider. A number of high-profile named horses could be mentioned here in all the disciplines. The skill of the 'new owner', the patience of that owner and the structure put in place between rider, coach and horse, will dictate how that new partnership evolves and what subsequent successes are achieved in the future. To consider that a 'schoolmaster' can be purchased and competing successfully with a new rider in a matter of weeks – or sometimes even months –is often a vain hope.

▶ EQUESTRIAN SCENARIO

Peter was training for his UKCC Level 3 and had a mentor-coach observing the session, where Peter was working with Shirley. Shirley was riding her fourteen-year-old Advanced dressage horse that she had purchased recently as a 'schoolmaster'. Shirley was a middle-aged lady with great aspirations to ride in top hat and tails; she had worked her way painstakingly through learning in a riding school, to owning her own cob with whom she had done

Riding Club level competitions and had lots of fun. Peter worked patiently with Shirley, asking her about what she wanted to achieve and gradually making an assessment of what Shirley did with her horse whilst working in. The working in was very variable. Shirley walked a while and then cantered. The canter became quite onward bound and the horse started to throw in flying changes at random as he was receiving little information from his rider. When Shirley returned to trot, there was a lot of power and expression from the horse and Shirley was often out of balance and then tended to rely too much on her reins. The rhythm was very intermittent and, despite Peter's best efforts to slow everything down to enable Shirley to regain control, and her own position and balance, she was obviously becoming frustrated as she got more tired. The session did not have a positive outcome, the rider having little to feel good about and the coach being frustrated by his own inability to help the partnership. The horse was confused and somewhat stressed.

After the session the mentor-coach spoke to Shirley and asked her: 'What was your aim today?' Her answer was 'I want to ride like Carl Hester.'

Speaking after the session, Peter told his mentor that he felt powerless to help a weak rider on a lovely knowledgeable horse that was getting very confused.

This scenario has many outcomes although sadly no beneficial ones for the horse in the current circumstances.

Let's consider the outcomes:

The horse

- This scopey, educated horse was, through no fault of his own, purchased to teach his loving owner all about Advanced dressage.

- His ability has been developed by a competent, coordinated, educated rider who had the skill to manage the range of movement and reaction of the horse. He was trained well and to a high standard. This meant that he had many movements that he could perform, depending on what 'buttons were pressed'.

- His new owner lacked all the skills of the previous rider. She lacked balance, coordination, timing, feel and knowledge. She had aspiration and aims in abundance (she wanted to ride like Carl Hester!) but these were totally unrealistic at this stage of her riding.

- When Shirley rode the horse, she had the image in her mind of how she wanted him to go, but none of the skills to make it happen.

- The horse felt mixed information being given and offered whatever he thought the aid being applied at any moment was asking for. His generosity often was 'rewarded' with rough treatment on his mouth.

- This only served to create a variety of flying changes in canter, much random variation in the trot rhythm and a confused, anxious horse.

The rider

- Excited by her new purchase and with a vision of what she would now be able to do with her 'schoolmaster', Shirley had overlooked the painstaking work she had put in to achieve her fun riding on her cob.

- While not frightened of the horse, Shirley had failed to recognise that the difference between the new horse and her trusty cob was similar to the difference between a Ferrari and a Land Rover. The high-powered horse was sensitive, reactive and powerful in a way that Shirley had little experience of.

- The rider would need a very structured and supportive plan to enable her to work towards her goal. This would need to start with a very frank and clear discussion between Shirley and her coach as to the small steps of progress that would enable her to maximise the ability of her lovely horse.

- It would be a challenging process, but not without a great deal of satisfying achievements along the way as long as both coach and learner were committed to the plan.

The coach

- Initially experienced much frustration at the outcome of the session.

- With frank self-reflection and open discussion with the rider about the issues, it should be easy to establish a satisfying and progressive plan of action.

Twelve months on:

- Horse and rider completed their first Advanced Medium test with no obvious mistakes. Shirley recognised how far she had come and was now aware of how much she had to work at developing the partnership with the horse to bring out his knowledge.

- The horse is now 'programmed' to Shirley's way of riding and Shirley has learnt to manage her balance, coordination, thinking, timing and preparation in a way that enables her horse to react in a sensitive and harmonious way because they can 'read each other'.

- Next stop is Advanced in 'top hat and tails'.

- Peter has learnt that this could never have been achieved without the rider taking ownership of her need to apply a structured and progressive plan of development. Having the 'golden goal' aim is only any good if the stepping stones can be put in place to reach it.

In conclusion on this subject, whether coach or rider, we must constantly 'read' the horses that we have the privilege to work with. We have the ultimate responsibility to ensure that our equine partners are willing and confident in their relationship with us and that our expectations of them are always based upon, and aimed for, with the maximum knowledge, empathy and consideration that our expertise allows. With horses we never stop learning, because every horse we are involved with has a slightly different temperament and ability (physical and mental) from the one before or after.

INSIGHTS

- The coach and rider will be more effective and skilful if they are *mindful* of themselves, others and their horse.

- We are hugely privileged to learn from every horse that we work with; they all teach us something new and different and so our 'horsemanship' is constantly evolving and developing.

- The horse weighs in the region of half a ton and if we forget that it will be at great risk to our own safety, that of others, and our well-being.

- The coach is a pivotal facilitator in the gradual establishment of a new relationship between a horse and rider.

- To maximise performance, the horse and rider must, at all times, be in secure and consistent communication and harmony.

- It is our responsibility, whether as coach or rider, to remember that the horse is generally a willing partner in what we ask of him, but we cannot expect him to react to the emotions, hopes, fears and aspirations that we have. He remains willing as long as, throughout our training, we treat him with respect and understanding and never 'humanise' him.

- Young riders must be encouraged to develop patience, timing and empathy with their horses to enable them to bring out the best in the partnership.

6. DELIVERY

POINT OF VIEW

As individuals we are all different, and therefore the coach needs to have a wide repertoire of interventions. Given the considerations and suggested reference points in the previous chapters, there are many different behavioural interventions that a coach could make. Therefore, it is probably safe to say that most of us do not have a repertoire that includes all of these options and possibilities!

A coach's overall approach should be relational not transactional, and the coach should be able to adapt their behaviour to a wide range of situations.

This chapter will outline the behaviours available to the coach and provide guidance on their appropriate application.

Coaching a technical skill requires knowledge, developing practical experience, passion, commitment and an ongoing desire to be better in your expertise than you were yesterday. It is not possible to be a perfect coach, but there will always be the aim and the potential to be a better coach. Some of the skills we have already discussed in this book, such as critical analysis and self-reflection, should be subjects that are constantly uppermost in the coach's and rider's mind as these skills ensure ongoing self-awareness and the ability to motivate and be self-starting. As riders we never stop learning

'There is a big difference between being a trainer and being a coach. Knowing when to switch from being one to being the other is an important key to getting the best out of riders. A good coach will never criticise failure but rather use the opportunity to analyse and learn from it. A coach should always be in the background, not in the foreground.'

CHRIS BARTLE FBHS, International rider and coach, trainer of German Event Team from our horses; they are our teachers. As coaches we are intrinsically linked to our riders and are therefore learning constantly from their experience with their horses.

OVERALL APPROACH: COACH-LED OR RIDER-LED?

This major decision point was introduced in Chapter 3. Here, we will explain it in more detail. From the first moment that a learner shows interest and curiosity in a subject, they begin to absorb knowledge about that subject. The brain is a very complex organ and, while the human brain can remember a one-off incident, consolidation of memory is through repetition and reinforcement of a pathway of practice. Just as our horses learn through repetition, so our brains store information through regular use of that pathway. As coaches, we need to ensure that riders takes the responsibility to 'learn' the information and it becomes imprinted on their brain, not ours! Once a new concept is introduced to a rider, whether that is a novice rider learning how to tighten the girth, or a more advanced rider learning how to maintain straightness in the canter prior to riding a flying change of leg, that information must be transferred to the learner's brain to ensure they have full ownership of it. A coach could often be heard saying 'I keep telling her to shorten her reins and she never does'. Until the rider takes responsibility for riding with shorter reins, no amount of 'telling' will make any difference, because it is the coach who is wanting the reins to be shorter, not the rider.

> 'Doing the same thing over and over again and expecting a different result is the definition of madness.'
>
> **ALBERT EINSTEIN**

▶ EQUESTRIAN SCENARIO

A number of years ago, at the British Equestrian Centre (BEC) at Stoneleigh, Warwickshire, a foreign rider/coach of international repute was giving a showjumping convention in front of a full capacity audience. The riders were young riders of national standard on up-and-coming horses of international potential. One rider constantly rode with long reins and the coach mentioned this on numerous occasions, with no obvious change from the rider. The rider approached a big oxer of about 1.40m from a corner; the horse completely missed his stride in the approach and the horse, rider and fence came crashing to the floor in a spectacular shambles. Six hundred people in the audience gasped in horror as horse, rider and the entire fence lay on the floor! The illustrious coach showed no sign of dismay at all; he turned his back on the carnage (horse and rider struggled to their feet with no apparent damage to either), walked slowly away shaking his head and saying very audibly 'I told her to shorten her reins'!

So what can we learn from this example?

- The rider was repeatedly 'told' to shorten her reins but this was not acted upon by the rider to the satisfaction of the coach.

- Why was this?
    - Did the rider not understand the request?
    - Did the rider not agree with the request, so did not carry it out?
    - Did the rider not believe or trust the coach, that this was a valid action to follow for improvement of performance?

- Was there discussion between rider and coach about this observation so that some or all of the above questions were addressed? On this occasion, 'No' to all these questions.

- If the coach observed no change in spite of his 'telling', why did he not change the method by which he was trying to encourage the rider to gain improvement through his coaching? Was there an alternative way to invite the rider to see that shortening her reins might change the outcome?

Then let's consider the spectacular mistake!

- Some would be quick to say that the accident should have been prevented.

- It is possible that there could have been injury to horse and/or rider and certainly, as coaches, we have a duty of care to avoid this happening.

- As coaches, we have a responsibility to always consider the risk involved in any session we are taking and minimise that risk.

- Should we prevent mistakes being made, because we have the expertise and knowledge to recognise the build-up to an incident and therefore stop the rider before they actually make the mistake?

- Consider the jumping rider in this scenario. Although it could be argued that other factors may have contributed to the mistake, if she realised that the major mistake she made at that fence was primarily a consequence of her not having her reins short enough, then she would learn from her mistake, which had been clearly and repeatedly identified by her coach. In that case the rider would take full responsibility for her action and its outcome and so learn conclusively that shortening her reins on the approach to a big fence could be a contributory factor to preventing the bad mistake she made.

If we constantly prevent riders from making mistakes of any kind, then we deny them the experience they gain from making those mistakes. The coach should avoid a style of teaching that always ensures the rider has a good experience. The rider who is always protected by the coach from things going wrong becomes comfortable in that 'good experience' and avoids anything that is outside that 'comfort zone'. Then, at a competition, the rider finds that their coach is no longer there to manage everything for them, and they are lacking the independent skills to deal with an unexpected situation in the ring. They thus fail in competition, which is the worst place to learn from their mistakes.

As coaches we do, however, have a duty of care to ensure that we *minimise* the risk taken in any situation in which we are in charge. Risk assessment is now a major consideration in all we do in life and, as trained coaches, we must always be able to confidently justify the choices we make in any coaching situation with our riders. We must show a clear pathway of judgement that led to the decision we made (in the case of the rider jumping the oxer, that would ensure her competence to complete the task with minimal risk to herself or the horse). Had the rider suffered a bad injury in this case, one doubts the coach would have been able to justify his decision to ask the rider to jump the fence safely, if he considered her reins were too long!

There is a benefit a rider derives from riding a variety of different horses, and every horse will teach the rider and coach something. Thinking from the outset of a learner's initial experience with riding, whether as a young child, an adolescent or an adult, there will be that development from the period of unconscious incompetence through to conscious incompetence (see page 80) and onward. The period of conscious incompetence may be lengthy, and often revisited throughout the riding experience. It is during this period where, for a learner, the relationship with the coach becomes pivotal in terms of the progress made and the management of the challenges that will arise inevitably and frequently.

The expertise of the coach will inevitably mean that aspects of each training session are coach-led. Whenever a rider needs to have technical input on a new subject (how to ride a movement, how to manage a resistance from the horse, etc.) the skills, competence and knowledge of the coach will lead the way in which the session is managed. The coach must educate the rider, by imparting and transferring their own expertise. It is this skill that singles out a great coach from a good coach. Any coach who can produce an athlete who is more successful, more able, more skilled than they themselves have been, is a highly competent coach indeed.

Moving from coach-led to rider-led style

As soon as the rider has grasped the basic concepts of a new piece of work, or resolved a problem that has required the coach to lead the training, the coach must show the adaptability to adjust their coaching style into a more rider-led approach. The rider must be encouraged to seize the initiative and take the work forward with independence and curiosity and explore and develop their competence. This ensures that the rider believes they have *achieved* the success, and will feel motivated to continue.

ADAPTABILITY

Involvement and adaptability are key here.

In any training session, remember that the session belongs to the learner. They are probably paying for the coach's skill and they, therefore, should be calling the tune.

Consider the scenario below.

▶ EQUESTRIAN SCENARIO

Katy is competing at Prix St Georges level; she has a competition coming up in the near future, in which she is trying out her new music and floor plan for the first time. She books a session with a coach from whom she has been trying to get a lesson for ages, but he is always really busy and his clinics are often full. This coach is expensive and there is a charge for the school hire as well, but Katy is optimistic that it will be money well spent, as she does not have a full-sized arena at home and really wants to try out the timing of her programme and music. Her session starts ten minutes later than the pre-booked time as the coach is running late; he then tells Katy to start warming up and takes a comfort break and answers his phone. There is no observation of the warming up routine and no introduction of himself to Katy, before the coach starts to work. He has not met or coached her before. Katy mentions that she has brought her music and would like a chance to run through it as she does not have a full-sized arena at home and the coach says 'Well, let's look at the work first, then we'll worry about the music.' The forty minutes are quickly used up with some fairly intensive trot and canter work, interspersed with the coach answering his phone and giving a few words of advice to another rider who has come into the school early to warm up. As time progresses and it is obvious that no more will be available to do what Katy had hoped to do with her horse, Katy gets frustrated and loses patience with her horse, and the horse's work deteriorates. The session ends exactly on the allotted time and the coach moves on to the next rider, who is clearly a rider he trains regularly.

This scenario shows up the following:

- A coach-led session where the rider was never involved at any stage.

- High expectation from the rider and also a clear plan of what the rider hoped to achieve from this particular training session.

- A certain lack of courtesy from the coach, running late at Katy's expense (time-wise and financially), answering his phone and taking a comfort break in Katy's time.

SELF-OBSESSED

- Complete lack of regard by the coach for Katy's aspirations for the session.

- An increasing disappointment from the rider as the session evolves and she is aware that, not only will her goals not be met, but neither will they even be discussed or valued.

- The inevitable effect that Katy's disappointment and state of mind about her lesson has on the partnership with her horse.

Every professional coach who is earning a living from coaching has a responsibility to ensure that every session is as valid to the learner as can be.

Developing rider-led sessions

The following are some guidelines for the equestrian coach:

- Be interested in every rider. They may have come to you because of your reputation, so make sure that they leave enhancing that reputation and speaking highly of you. Know their name and find out what they hope to achieve. You may consider that their aims are totally unrealistic, but it is through your skill as a coach that they learn, recognise and accept that – not just through you telling them!

- Discuss what they are going to show you and then watch them show you! A rider's horse may or may not be warmed up and that again is an area for discussion. For example, 'Is that how he normally works'? 'Would you usually take a longer warm-up'?

- Discuss what you have seen, what you like – they will want your opinion of what they have shown you; they will want to know what you think of them and their horse. Then discuss the shortcomings. Ask, discuss, invite – don't just tell!

- If all you do is 'tell', then you are making assumptions about what you have seen; you give no opportunity for input or feedback from the rider and they cannot then feel involved.

- Of course, as a highly skilled coach (or even as a less-experienced coach) you have 'seen it all before', but empowering the rider will only ever happen if you allow the rider's input.

- Questions and obtaining feedback are two of the most powerful coaching skills that you can develop and they must become an integral part of every coaching session at whatever level you teach. If you do not question, how will you ever know what information has been stored in the rider's brain? If you do not question, how will you know what your rider understands? If you do not question, how do you know their state of mind?

- Deciding on the plan of work in each session should be built on input from the rider, observation of the horse's way of going, time, fitness of horse and rider, facilities and technical expertise of the coach.

- Satisfaction for the rider will lead to increased harmony with their partnership with the horse.

- If the rider understands, feels confident, feels secure and trusts the coach, then the outcome is likely to be much more harmonious.

- If the rider is confused or unclear, feels nervous and insecure in their control of the horse, is anxious that the coach may ask more of them than they feel able to give, the partnership is likely to be tense and inconsistent.

Rider-led coaching sessions do not mean that the coach abdicates all responsibility for developing the rider's skill, knowledge and competence. Rather, they demonstrate an adaptability and skill in the coach, to bring out the best of every rider through communication, involvement and feedback, which empower the rider to maximise their skill in a confident, evolving way.

QUESTIONS, QUESTIONS, QUESTIONS . . .

Questions are one of the most valuable tools when coaching. 'Why did the apple fall to the ground from the tree?' (Sir Isaac Newton.) 'What is beyond that horizon? Will I fall off the end of the world?' (Christopher Columbus pioneering navigation and 'finding' the New World.)

So, although this skill sits within the behavioural model that will be introduced later in this chapter, we have chosen to give it special prominence below.

People are curious about their surroundings; it is that curiosity that makes them explore their world, question their parameters, and motivates them to expand their boundaries. For both coaches and learners, curiosity through questioning is powerful and, if repressed, it will inhibit learning. Sometimes experience leads to a tendency for coaches to tell learners 'This is the way to do it' and 'Believe me, I know from years of experience, so listen and learn.' That can be laudable, but if coaches repress curiosity or questioning from the learner, they inadvertently close a valuable avenue of self-discovery and ingenuity. That ingenuity could produce resourcefulness, initiative and originality, resulting in a powerful competitor, enabled by the skill and creativity of both learner and coach. This is what we have seen in the development of the outstanding relationship between the skill of Carl Hester MBE, FBHS (who wrote the foreword for this book) as coach, and the exceptional talent of his protégé Charlotte Dujardin OBE.

Questions in coaching and learning are tools, and any tool can be either well used, creating good results, or badly managed producing equally bad, destructive outcomes.

▶EQUESTRIAN SCENARIO

Some years ago a well-known senior instructor was delivering a seminar to a group of young and aspiring instructors. After an active morning of the instructor demonstrating her techniques there was a short question and answer session prior to the lunch break. One young instructor asked a question. The immediate, sharp response from the seminar leader was: 'That is the most basic question imaginable. If you don't know the answer to that then you should be ashamed of yourself and I am not even going to demean you further by answering it'! There was an 'audible silence' and shrinking by the other delegates present and, after the lunch break, half the delegates did not return for the afternoon's session.

What did this situation demonstrate?

• The leader of the course had no idea of the destructive effect that her one reply had, not only on the questioner but on the other attendees.

• The response given by the leader ensured that the rest of the delegates were not going to ask any questions, in case they too received a denigrating reply.

• This course leader also ensured that, on future occasions, attendees would be reluctant to get involved through questioning and discussion, in case they were perceived as being weak in their knowledge.

• With one swift and sharp ill-thought-out response, this course leader ensured equally swift transference of the way she had treated one delegate, to a large number of that delegate's peer group.

The following statement comes to mind here: 'After an event a person quickly forgets the words that have been said to them – however it takes a long time before they forget how those words made them feel!'

A coach needs to use words with due care and a perception of how they may make the learner feel. Discussion and questioning will ensure clarity and help to avoid the damage that can be done by assuming knowledge. Always consider the perception that a learner may be developing, evolving an opinion about you, the coach. This perception is formulated by the way you develop your relationship with the learner. Always demonstrate respect, interest, willingness to communicate, involvement and an obvious genuine desire to help and improve their skill.

Questions as communication

Questions can be used to build a powerful communication between coach and learner, learner and coach, if they are used appropriately.

- With confidence and forethought.

- Those asked by the coach need sensitivity, clarity and tact.

- Open questions invite thinking and depth of reply.

- How, what, when, why, are words that encourage an individual response, but also one that encourages the learner to think.

- A small question initially can then be expanded after a response to develop the thinking and to further motivate and inspire the learner.

- Avoid using 'why' questions (see Exploring, page 175).

- Questions should be used with skill, timing, depth and sincerity.

- Ultimately the skill and involvement of the coach as questioner, combined with the knowledge expressed by the learner through their answers, should dictate the development of the next stage of training offered by the coach.

The coach needs to have an awareness of the learner's ability to answer the question (this may confirm understanding or knowledge of a subject). If an answer is not readily forthcoming, then the coach must be able to adapt the question swiftly and proficiently to encourage or elicit an answer that allows the learner to feel achievement.

To use questions appropriate to the level of competence of the learner, and in such a way that the next stage of training can be planned, the coach must listen to the learner's response. We all fall into the trap of 'hearing' (we are bombarded by sound around us all the time), but to really listen requires a separate set of skills, such as involvement, body language, encouragement, prompting, expenditure of time.

We are often guilty of short-cutting responses to questions, such as second guessing, or even answering the question we have asked with our own reply, if the learner is not quick to reply themselves. It is important to remember that the learner's response is essential feedback.

Adaptability is a key attribute and skill for a coach, moving to and from rider-led to coach-led scenarios as appropriate. Your ongoing ability as a coach to monitor your own delivery to the learner is essential. Throughout any session, you must be able to recognise and assess your learner's response to your delivery. If your method of delivery is not obviously achieving an improvement, then you need to consider the following:

- Does your learner understand what you are trying to put across?

- Is there confusion or lack of agreement from your learner?

- Have you asked questions to explore what your learner is thinking or feeling?

Have you pressed on regardless, convinced that 'you are right'? This can then develop into a loss of confidence and deterioration in the relationship, if your learner is of another opinion.

Here, *your* adaptability may be the key to progress. Be prepared to change your style of delivery in order to assist your learner's understanding.

THE COACHING DELIVERY PROCESS

We would suggest the following seven stages in the delivery process.

Step 1: contracting

This part of the process includes agreeing ground rules on what the coaching will include and how the partnership between the coach and learner is going to operate. It is useful to have an explicit discussion on roles and responsibilities. A great coach will not create dependency, and one of the reasons for contracting formally with the learner is to ensure that the ownership and responsibility for self-development clearly rests with the learner.

A joint agreement between learner and coach might include both tangible and intangible elements:

Tangible

- Logistics.

- Time-keeping.

- Reviews with honest discussions about progress (or lack of it) .

- Payment terms.

- Cancellation policy (fees may be involved if an arena was booked or travel time has been incurred).

- Frequency of sessions.

Intangible

- Confidentiality.

- Depth and breadth of delivery.

- Mutual trust and respect.

- Feedback.

- Commitment.

In summary, both parties need to discuss and agree what needs to be worked on and how.

Step 2: assessing the situation – level of coaching required

An equestrian coach will need to assess very quickly at the beginning of each session where they should focus their attention. Is the rider dealing with a one-off, short-term challenge – requiring a **tactical intervention**, or a problem that has happened a few times – requiring a **strategic intervention**, or is the rider experiencing a pattern of outcomes which are not working and therefore a **transformational shift** is required? Tactical coaching could deal with a horse and rider who are unsettled by some unusually bad weather; strategic coaching might help a rider with their general approach to jumps (for example, they don't prepare well enough); transformational coaching would be needed when a rider is making the same mistakes every time, which are fear-based (for example, an event rider who is brave most of

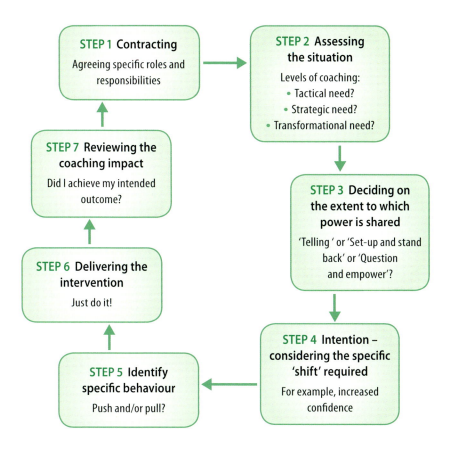

The delivery process.

the time but struggles with very large open spaces owing to a horse having bolted with them on a previous occasion). In summary:

Tactical: A one-off issue/situation

Strategic: A theme is emerging

Transformation: A pattern of behaviour has become engrained

Step 3: the extent to which power is shared – the power continuum

As coaches we have a fundamental decision point regarding the extent to which we share power and control with the learner. Moving to the right of the continuum will create a more empowered environment and provide a platform for transformational development.

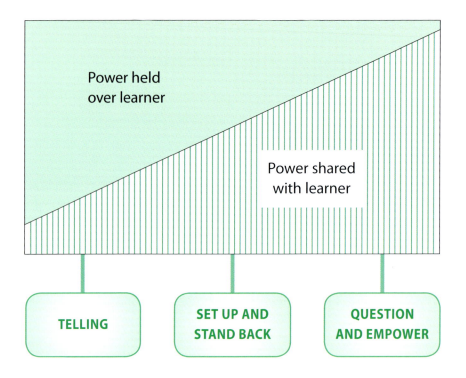

The power continuum.

Often a coach who likes '*telling*' the rider what to do all the time, will come back with the argument that they know best and asking the rider's opinion just wastes time. However, if the rider's feedback is never invited, how will the coach know what they are thinking and what knowledge they are taking on board?

There are, however, many occasions when 'telling' is very necessary:

- When the rider needs to know what a new movement is. For example, when teaching leg-yielding for the first time, the rider must know what the movement involves and what the aids are for leg-yielding. This is a '**tell**' situation.

- When making a correction of a movement. For example, if there is too much neck bend in shoulder-in, the rider must know what to do to make the correction. This is a '**tell**' situation.

- In an emergency. For example, if the horse bucks or spooks violently there may be a need to instantly '**tell**' the rider what to do to manage.

There are many times when '**telling**' can be exchanged for '**set up and stand back**', as in the following example:

- You, as coach, told the rider what leg-yielding was and what the aids were and they rode it with some help from you on the left rein.

- Now, on the other rein, invite the rider to go and try the same exercise in the other direction. Watch them ride it (with minimal help if possible) and then ask for feedback. This is '**setting up and standing back**'; allowing the rider to find out for themselves what they can do. Even if they find it difficult, give them minimal prompting and encourage them to try for themselves. Sometimes they will say they have forgotten how to do it, in which case remind them and let them try – you are still '**setting up and standing back**'.

- Questioning after letting them try is then directed at finding out how much they have taken on board about 'doing the exercise'.

This feedback from the work is '**questioning and empowering the rider**'.

- Well-selected questions to the rider will then encourage the rider to think about what they felt and what they found easy/difficult.

- If the rider answers 'I don't know' to a question, do not be tempted to give them the answer. Send them out to ride the exercise or work again with one or two specific directives to think about. They should then think through the work relating to the points you directed them towards. Then you '**question and empower**' on their return.

- This will encourage the rider to think and try harder. You are '**empowering them**'.

As a coach, you will find that, in order to educate effectively, you are constantly using a 'sliding scale' of delivery techniques. Sometimes you are '**telling**' the rider, sometimes '**setting up and standing back**' and sometimes '**questioning and empowering**'. You are also recognising the rider's learning style when they say to you 'Oh I see what you mean' (visual learner), or 'Yes I could feel that' (kinaesthetic learner) or 'Could you explain the aids for that movement?' (auditory/theorist learner).

The following are two examples from a corporate/business environment.

▶ CORPORATE SCENARIO 1

A business executive is finding it hard to prioritise their work and, as a result, starts to miss deadlines and let others down, including customers. The coach creates a template for the executive which outlines when they should do what within a working week (based on some assumptions about a 'standard' week). The executive has some success with this approach but it doesn't allow for the fluid and changing nature of the business environment. The template may have worked in other situations but is too generic and therefore doesn't meet the specific needs of the executive. The executive's frustration and stress levels are increasing by the day, so the coach recommends a book on time management. The executive is not sure where they will find the time to read the book, and therefore asks the coach for some immediate solutions. The coach tells the executive that they need to recruit a good PA. Unfortunately, it later transpires that there is no budget for additional head count. The executive concludes wrongly that their environment needs to change in order to solve their problem, so resigns from their job. As they have not addressed their own ability to prioritise, and create realistic plans, their frustration will continue, and performance will drop.

▶ CORPORATE SCENARIO 2

The coach explores with the business executive their role, scope of responsibilities, and the calibre of their team – to what extent are there people to whom they can delegate? The coach invites the executive to keep a diary after the first session and before the next meeting to more fully understand where they are choosing to focus their time and effort. Also, the executive is encouraged to research the strategy of their organisation, including future business opportunities. Other actions between sessions include 1:1 discussions with their direct reports (those who work directly to them) to establish to what extent they are ready, willing and able to take more responsibility. The executive is encouraged to come to the next coaching discussion with some ideas and possible actions.

The coach will sometimes need to 'tell' a learner what to do, especially if they lack the confidence and competence necessary for the task, or there is some 'danger' if the learner doesn't quickly act in a different way. However, this approach can breed too much dependency on the coach.

'**Set up and stand back**' in a business environment could include observing the executive at work with their team, and then making some suggestions as to how they might change their leadership style. The learner should be encouraged to try out 'useful experiments', where they take an idea from the coach, but they are responsible for the action.

'**Question and empower**' can work particularly well when the learner has forgotten past success. The executive in the scenario has competence and experience, but is lacking confidence in a new situation. Questions help stimulate the learner's thinking – tapping into a human being's innate ability to problem-solve.

*It can be dangerous for a coach in the corporate world to '**tell**' an executive what to do.* If the actions are implemented they could have 'unintended negative consequences' e.g. legal, budgetary and reputational implications. However, '**telling**' can be useful when:

- The executive is overwhelmed and cannot see a way forward.

- The executive needs to stop doing something that would be damaging to themselves and others.

- The executive has an immediate dilemma that needs resolving quickly, for example two very demanding and aggressive customers wanting a meeting at the same time on the same day.

'**Set up and stand back**' in a business environment can encourage the learner to take more responsibility for their situation. It is not helpful for the learner to become dependent on the coach, as they will not be there forever! This approach can be summarised thus:

- Coach highlights to the executive the implications of ongoing stress.

- Coach invites the executive to research the possibility of more funding for resources.

- Coach suggests that they delegate more tasks to a few high-calibre direct reports.

'**Question and empower**' in a business environment can be summarised as follows:

- Coach poses well-crafted, focused and specific questions to explore what is troubling the executive.

- There is a discussion about what organisational blocks could prevent a change in procedures and processes.

- The executive is encouraged to seek feedback (informally and formally) from their manager and trusted colleagues on their performance. Friends and family members may also be able to offer a useful and insightful perspective.

Step 4: intention – what specific shift is required?

We would advocate that the coach needs to determine their intention, before they consider their behaviour: 'What am I trying to achieve, what is the outcome I'm aiming for?' 'What needs to be different in and with the learner for them to succeed?' It could be:

- Mindset

- Confidence

- Knowledge

- Experience

- Attitude

- Skill

- Emotional resilience

- Breaking a personal block

- Motivation

- Focus and direction (goals) and/or

- Feelings.

INTENTION + BEHAVIOUR = IMPACT

The coach's intention should inform their intervention style, whilst also considering the way the learner interacts, for example, do they like lots of facts and information? If there are feelings getting in the way, these will need to be explored *before* a suggestion is made. John Heron, of the Human Potential Research Project at Surrey University, identified six categories of intervention, as shown below.

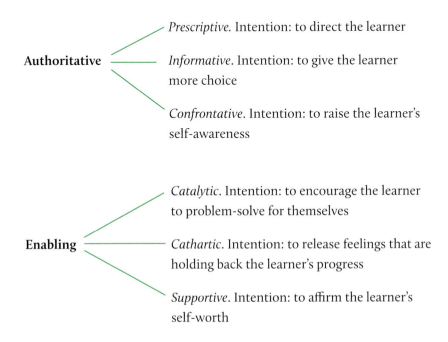

Authoritative

Prescriptive. Intention: to direct the learner

Informative. Intention: to give the learner more choice

Confrontative. Intention: to raise the learner's self-awareness

Enabling

Catalytic. Intention: to encourage the learner to problem-solve for themselves

Cathartic. Intention: to release feelings that are holding back the learner's progress

Supportive. Intention: to affirm the learner's self-worth

The correct use and application of the styles will create the following outcomes:

Prescriptive ⟶ New direction and/or sense of purpose

Informative ⟶ New possibilities and choices

Confrontative ⟶ Increased ownership and commitment

Catalytic ⟶ Induce self problem-solving

Cathartic ⟶ New, more positive feelings

Supportive ⟶ Improved self-confidence

Heron's model is a particularly powerful tool for helping coaches be clear and discerning about their *intentions* and desired *outcomes* from the specific coaching intervention.

It is important to understand that these six categories are more about your *intention* as a coach, rather than the specific behaviours you could use. So, for example, an open question could fall into any of the categories depending on the degree of trust in the relationship, the non-verbal behaviours used, the context, and the learner's receptivity. Below is an overview of the six categories.

Authoritative

Prescriptive

Giving best advice, offering opinion, reviewing performance. A prescriptive intervention is one that explicitly seeks to direct the behaviour of the learner.

Example: 'I think it would be useful for you to do a test-riding clinic in order to assess your readiness for the next level of competition. Then you can make a plan as to which competitions to enter.'

Issues:

How much advice to give.

Whether to give any advice at all.

Creating dependency in the learner.

Informative

Giving information, imparting knowledge, offering interpretation, providing non-evaluative feedback. An informative intervention seeks to impart new knowledge and information to the learner.

Example: 'From my experience, it is always advantageous to involve your coach when buying a new horse.'

Issues:

Overdoing it. Boring the learner.

Confrontative

Being challenging, giving direct feedback. A confronting intervention directly challenges the restrictive attitude/belief/behaviour of the learner, that is, they are limiting themselves and, in equestrian contexts, probably the horse.

Example: 'My impression is that you are avoiding having a difficult conversation with your sponsor, who has let you down.'

Issues:

Too much too soon. Aggressive interventions triggered by anxiety in the coach. Poor judgement and/or perception of the learner.

Enabling

Catalytic

Encouraging self-directed problem-solving, eliciting information. A catalytic intervention seeks to enable the learner to learn and develop through self-direction and by self-discovery within the context of the coach-learner situation, but also potentially beyond it.

Example: 'What's holding you back with your horse, as you seem quite tentative in your riding?'

Issues:

Embarrassing the learner because they truly don't know what to do next. Using leading questions which sound more like a prescription rather than encouraging the learner to problem-solve and analyse themselves.

THE COACH AS CATALYST

Cathartic

Releasing tension, encouraging laughter/crying/trembling/storming. A cathartic intervention seeks to enable the learner to discharge painful emotion, thereby 'letting go' of feelings.

Example: 'You say that you're feeling relaxed about the show, but you appear rather anxious ...'

Issues:

Being seen as intrusive, which is more likely if there is no implicit or explicit agreement to discuss personal feelings.

Choosing the time and place to explore feelings.

Supportive

Being approving/confirming/validating. A supportive intervention affirms the worth and value of the learner and increases their confidence.

Example: 'I know that you can achieve this goal based on your past determination and skill level.'

Issues:

Colluding with the learner, if the coach is too supportive.

Promoting too much confidence in the absence of competence.

John Heron regards his list as exhaustive in that all positive interventions can be interpreted using the six-category model – although there may sometimes be an overlap between categories since they are, to some extent, interdependent.

> 'For me, the real revelation was having a really engaging trainer. I can always remember so strongly the moment when I really "got" collection from canter into walk; this is such a vital basic to have at FEI level, with the simple changes being a key element. I was eleven at the time and was riding my pony Hillmen in the arena with Peter (Storr) on his Small Tour horse; he talked me through exactly how to do it and demonstrated by cantering his horse next to my pony, who was only walking! Having a trainer show you how to do something as well as tell you is a huge benefit. I've been very lucky to have the privilege of training with and watching Peter ride over the years.'
>
> **PHOEBE PETERS,** European Pony Dressage Champion gold medallist

Step 5: specific coaching behaviours

Within all of these approaches there will need to be a degree of 'push and pull'. 'Push energy' is where the coach draws on their own knowledge, experience and ideas to guide the learner. This energy converts into **assertive styles**. 'Pull energy' is where the coach encourages the learner to use themselves as the catalyst for change. This energy converts into **responsive styles**. Resources will be maximised if the coach shares their knowledge and ideas, and *also* values the learner's contribution. In addition to 'push and pull' energies, individuals may find themselves on the receiving end of 'fight or flight' energies. These convert into aggressive and passive behaviours, which have no place in a learning environment.

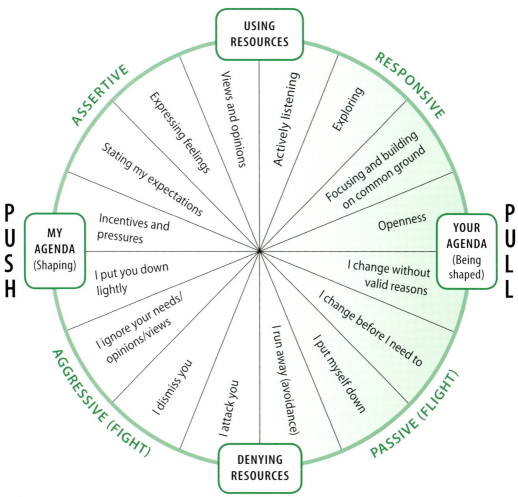

Behavioural styles.

A coach who thinks they are always right, has one preferred mode, and doesn't invest in their own development, will probably be seen as a dinosaur! In relation to the adjacent behavioural model, we recommend that a coach uses *only* a combination of styles in the top half.

It will be seen from the diagram that there are four **'assertive'** (push) styles, and four **'responsive'** (pull) styles. The **assertive** styles include: 'views and opinions'; expressing feelings'; 'stating expectations'; and 'incentives and pressures'. The **responsive** styles include: 'active listening'; 'exploring'; 'common ground'; and 'openness'. *The behaviours on the bottom half of the model should be avoided.* The next diagram highlights some of the micro-behaviours within each of the push and pull styles.

'PUSH' ENERGY
ASSERTIVE

'PULL' ENERGY
RESPONSIVE

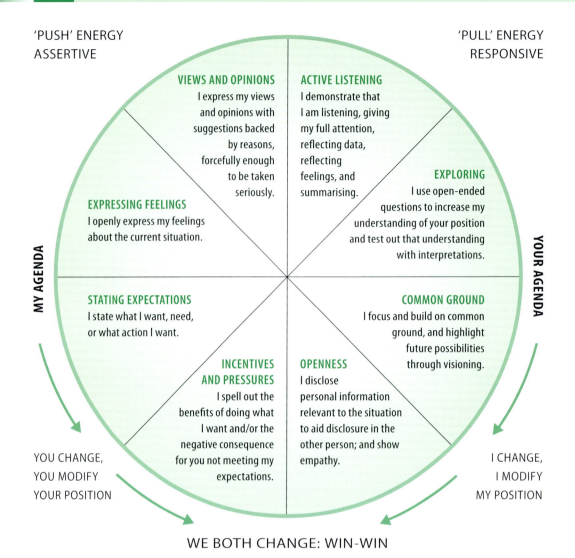

MY AGENDA

YOUR AGENDA

VIEWS AND OPINIONS
I express my views and opinions with suggestions backed by reasons, forcefully enough to be taken seriously.

ACTIVE LISTENING
I demonstrate that I am listening, giving my full attention, reflecting data, reflecting feelings, and summarising.

EXPLORING
I use open-ended questions to increase my understanding of your position and test out that understanding with interpretations.

EXPRESSING FEELINGS
I openly express my feelings about the current situation.

STATING EXPECTATIONS
I state what I want, need, or what action I want.

COMMON GROUND
I focus and build on common ground, and highlight future possibilities through visioning.

INCENTIVES AND PRESSURES
I spell out the benefits of doing what I want and/or the negative consequence for you not meeting my expectations.

OPENNESS
I disclose personal information relevant to the situation to aid disclosure in the other person; and show empathy.

YOU CHANGE,
YOU MODIFY
YOUR POSITION

I CHANGE,
I MODIFY
MY POSITION

WE BOTH CHANGE: WIN-WIN

Positive coaching styles.

So, there are eight styles in all that we would advocate, although the combination of behaviours and the degree to which they are used should depend entirely on the situation.

For maximum impact and in order to avoid confusion, there needs to be congruency in the delivery. Do the 'words' (language), 'music' (voice tone), and 'dance' (body language) convey the same message? For example, if an open-ended question is intended to understand the learner's thoughts and feelings in order to empower them, but the voice tone is judgemental, the desired outcome will not be achieved. The words and music may be in sync, but a raised eyebrow could completely change the message where there is a mixture of 'push' and 'pull' in one statement or question – this will come across as a 'push-me-pull you', leading to misunderstandings between the coach and learner. If there is a mixed message, we are more likely to believe the body language of the messenger, than other signals.

Step 6: 'Just do it'

This is the point at which the coach delivers the coaching. We believe that if the coach has considered all the elements suggested in the previous steps, then the impact will be more productive, constructive and legitimate.

Step 7: 'Review'

The coach should notice the impact of their behaviour – has it achieved the intended outcome? If it's not obvious as to how helpful or not the coaching has been, the coach should be pre-pared to explore the learner's reaction. The coach must then be prepared to change potentially their overall approach and/or specific style.

'Sometimes we need to push forward with the training; on other occasions it is time to back off/consolidate.'

NICK BURTON, GBR World Class Programme dressage coach for eventing, Performance Manager for dressage and eventing for The Hong Kong Jockey Club, FEI/Olympic level judge for eventing, List 1 FEI dressage judge

'Words', 'music' and 'dance' guidelines for each coaching style

Expressing views and opinions

Words: 'It seems to me …', 'I strongly recommend …', 'In my view …', 'I believe …', 'I think that …', 'I suggest …', 'The data implies …', 'Because …', 'My reasons are, first …'.

Music: Calm, logical, even-paced, with conviction but not over-forceful; rational not emotional.

Dance: Confident, upright, good eye contact.

Example: 'I suggest that we agree a schedule of coaching sessions now for the next three months, in order to protect the time.'

This style works best when the learner needs guidance, the coach has more relevant experience, and the learner responds well to facts and data.

Expressing feelings

Words: 'Right now I feel ...' (emotion), 'I am ...' (emotion).

'About ...' (situation).

'Because ...' (description of other person/peoples' behaviour).

Music: Firm, direct, congruent with the emotion being expressed.

Dance: Upright, confident, strong eye contact.

Example: 'I'm frustrated that you have not practised at all since our last session.'

This style works best when the coach has authentic emotions about the situation, for example, health and safety, and needs to add more weight to their basic assertion, such as a proposal.

Stating expectations

Words: 'I want ...', 'I need ...', 'I expect ...'.

Music: Determined, firm.

Dance: Feet firmly planted on the floor, upright, strong eye contact, firm hand gestures.

Example: 'I want you to take the same cross-country jump again but with more preparation and less speed this time.'

This style works best when the learner needs to be challenged, especially if they are not responding to logic and information. Also, this approach is legitimate if the learner is involved in a repetitive situation and there is an urgent need for a decision or action.

Incentives and pressures

Words: 'If you do ...', 'I will do ...', and/or 'If you don't do ... I will do ...'.

Music: Strong – forceful if necessary.

Dance: Confident, rooted.

Example: 'I want you to stop using your stick and spurs on the horse – the mistakes so far have been all yours. If you do this, I will be

> happy to continue the coaching session but if you insist on punishing the horse inappropriately then you will need to find another coach.'

This style works best when there is a serious issue at stake and where there will be genuine consequences if the learner does not change their behaviour, for example, horse welfare.

Active listening

Words: 'So what you're saying is ...', 'Let me check my understanding ...', 'You sound angry about that ...'.

Music: Encouraging, empathetic, matches the energy of the speaker.

Dance: Good eye contact, body position matching that of the speaker.

Example: 'My interpretation from your comments is that you trust your horse, but are questioning your own ability.'

This style works best when the learner has relevant knowledge, ideas and experience which could be endorsed by the coach.

Exploring

Words: 'Tell me about ...', 'How did you ...?', 'What happened then ...?', 'When did ...?', 'Which of those is the most important to you ...?'

Music: Encouraging, warm.

Dance: Good eye contact, matching that of the speaker.

Example: 'What are you taking away from today's coaching session'?

This style works best when there's a need to get 'under the skin' of the learner and engage them more fully in order to gain commitment to their learning. However, 'why' questions should be avoided, as the learner may become defensive because they feel the need to justify a stance. (See page 156–8 for more examples of this skill.)

Focusing and building on common ground

Words: 'So we're agreed that ...', 'I agree with you ...', 'Let's see what we do agree on ...', 'It's rather like ...', 'Just imagine ...', 'I can see us now ...'.

Music: Positive, enthusiastic, interesting.

Dance: Lively, animated.

Example: 'We both want the best for your new young horse – with the right training I could see you winning lots of competitions all the way to the top.'

This style works best when the coach wants to build a positive learning environment and engage the learner emotionally in the exciting possibilities of the future. This is the most appropriate behaviour if the learner needs to be inspired.

Openness

Words: Words appropriate to the disclosure, for example: 'I'm a bit confused ...','I'd like to be open about ...', 'I'd appreciate your help ...', 'I'm going to find this hard to say ...', 'The way I've been looking at it is ...'.

Music: Sincere, warm, non-defensive.

Dance: Open gestures, eye contact.

Example: 'My impression is that you're not comfortable with my approach.'

This style works best when there is a need to build trust in the relationship and show support through empathy.

Delivery caveats

The overuse or under-use of any coaching behaviour on its own is likely to have a negative impact, as shown in the accompanying diagram.

High views and opinions	Dogmatic/over-opinionated?
Low views and opinions	Fence-sitter/Easily swayed?
High expressing feelings	Over-emotional/Uncontrolled?
Low stating expectations	Unclear/Under-demanding?
High incentives and pressures	Too heavy too soon or too often?
Low incentives and pressures	Not prepared to bargain?
High active listening	Putting other's position as more important than own
Low active listening	Under-valuing the other's position/ point of view?
High exploring	Interrogative/Intrusive?
Low exploring	Not interested in the other person's position? Take too much at face value?
High common ground	Superficial if other 'pull 'behaviours are low i.e. no depth
Low common ground	Focusing mainly on differences?
High openness	Transparent/Vulnerable?
Low openness	Low levels of trust?

The consequences following the underuse or overuse of the coaching styles.

Unfortunately, even if, in the moment, the coach uses assertive styles in an appropriate way, the impact over time could be one of aggression, whereby the learner feels that their own thoughts and feelings are not valued. Equally, if the responsive styles are primarily used, albeit in a constructive way, the perception in the longer term could be one of passivity. For example, the coach may be viewed as 'sitting on the fence'!

Avoiding negatives

Below are examples of negative behaviours which should be avoided.

The coach changes without valid reasons. The coach feels intimidated by the rider so backs down before thinking through the implications of changing their mind.
Example: 'Perhaps you're right, you know your horse best.'

The coach changes before they need to. The coach misinterprets the rider's response, as they think they see dissatisfaction and change their view too quickly with no discussion.
Example: 'Ok, that didn't work so let's try it your way.'

The coach puts themselves down. The coach lacks confidence and uses too many qualifiers.
Example: 'I just wanted to test the horse's ability over a higher fence ... I'm sorry that I've got it wrong again.'

The coach runs away (avoidance). The coach finds the rider too resistant and so avoids the difficult conversation.
Example: 'You're doing really well' (even if they're not).

The coach puts the rider down lightly. The coach may use humour inappropriately and/or be trying to take a 'one-up' position.
Example: 'You look like a sack of potatoes on that horse.'

The coach ignores the rider's needs/opinions/views. The coach doesn't listen enough to the rider, and takes a patronising stance.
Example: 'Look, I've been riding and coaching much longer than you so you should listen to my advice ... keep going even though you're saying that you are tired.'

The coach dismisses the rider. The coach takes an arrogant position.
Example: I'm not interested in your opinion as you are a lousy rider.'

The coach attacks the rider. The coach shows aggressive behaviour by backing the rider into a corner.

Example: You are being an idiot, and others are embarrassed watching you. I suggest you give up riding.'

RECEIVING AND GIVING FEEDBACK

This is a specific skill within the style of 'views and opinions'. To facilitate development, improvement and expertise, whether as coach or learner, there needs to be feedback. Feedback is the delivery of accurate, appropriate and constructive information, based on observation of an activity or performance, which can then provide analysis and evaluation for future action.

Initially we think of feedback in categories of criticism or praise, but basic advice and guided self-discovery (the coach uses listening and questioning skills to develop opinions) can also be useful sources of feedback.

Let's consider the receiving and giving of feedback separately and then find common ground from perceptions of both.

Receiving feedback

The acceptance of the feedback you receive may vary according to who is delivering the information to you and what level of knowledge and expertise you have in comparison to the deliverer of the feedback.

When you receive feedback from another person do you:

- Listen actively to their description?

- Consider what you hear and try to see it from their viewpoint?

- Consider the pros and cons of the information?

- Agree mutually that there are points for discussion?

- Defend every point of criticism and justify your reason for your actions?

- Dismiss their opinions as not being appropriate to what you were demonstrating?

- Indicate that your experience is greater than theirs and, on that basis you do not value their input?

Giving feedback

There are strategies that can be adopted to ensure that feedback is given in such a way that it becomes a key to facilitating the coach's development.

The timing of when feedback is given can be crucial in ensuring that the coach or learner receiving the feedback accepts it with a positive and self-reflective frame of mind.

Feedback should be given as soon after the event as possible, while the activity is still fresh in the mind of the deliverer, then key points can be tactfully drawn out or referred to, and self-evaluation and self-reflection are more likely to occur and be honest.

It is preferable that feedback is given in a 'comfortable' environment (not in a howling gale, outside in the rain or cold, or where there are too many people around).

Especially if there is negative feedback to be delivered, it is important to balance the negative messages with some positive points, if possible. It is essential that the key points of weakness are highlighted and not embellished in any way that would enable the receiver to deflect the 'blame' away from their lack of competence.

▶EQUESTRIAN SCENARIO

Christopher is receiving feedback from the assessor of the group lesson he has just completed in taking his UKCC Level 2. The two examples below will demonstrate good and not so good feedback. In each example, we have used 'A' for the assessor, and 'C' for Christopher.

Good feedback

A 'Please sit down Christopher. How did you feel your lesson went?'

C 'I thought it was okay?' (Questioning tone and tentative body language hoping that A agrees.)

A 'Tell me what you thought of the level of both riders.'

C 'Well, they were okay.'

A 'Tell me what your main aim was after you had assessed them.'

C 'I just worked to improve them.'

A 'What did you think were the key weaknesses of rider No 1. that needed help?'

C 'Well, I suppose her aids weren't very good'.

A 'What did you think her knowledge of correct diagonals in trot was?'

C 'Well, I didn't really notice that, I wanted to teach them about suppleness and contact in transitions but neither of them was very good.'

A 'What did the riders want to work on?'

C 'I don't know really, but the goal was to work on suppleness and transitions.'

A 'Was that your goal or the riders' goal?'

C 'They didn't know enough to choose a goal and that's what I was told to coach.'

A 'I'm sorry that on this occasion Christopher you have not been successful in demonstrating the skills required at Level 2.'

C 'Well I kept them busy and they said they enjoyed it.'

A 'I am sorry Christopher but today I am unable to pass you for this assessment. You have a pleasant manner and a good, clear voice and you showed control of the riders throughout the session. Today however, you needed to show ability to assess the riders and choose an area of their weakness that you could help them with, within the brief of 'suppleness and contact in transitions'. There needed to be clearer discussion with your riders as to what they felt their strengths and weaknesses were and what they would like to work on in the session. There needed to be more help with their basic positions and awareness of aid application and diagonals so that this could link to their ability to ride their horses in a good rhythm and forward in the gaits. This, in turn, would help the suppleness and contact in transitions.

It would have helped you to establish more rapport with your riders if you had asked them some questions from time to time to find out what information they were taking from you. This would also have given them and the horses a rest from time to time. You need to consider these areas that you need to work on and I wish you luck the next time you take the assessment. Is there anything you feel you want to ask me? I will note the following points on the form I am going to give you and, when you have read them, feel free to come back and discuss them with me.'

Weak feedback

A 'Please sit down Christopher and tell me how your lesson went.'

C 'I thought it was okay?' (Questioning tone.)

A 'Well, you had two fairly weak riders didn't you, but tell me about their knowledge of diagonals.'

C 'I wasn't concentrating on that, as my brief was to teach about suppleness and contact in transitions.'

A 'When you assessed them, what did you think the main fault was with each rider?'

C 'I was disappointed they were both so weak, I didn't think I could demonstrate my coaching well because they weren't as good as I thought they would be.'

A (Laughing) 'Yes, they were a bit insecure weren't they. There was the time when the one horse spooked: what did you tell the rider then to help her?'

C 'She wasn't listening because there was a commotion outside and that's what caused the horse to spook.'

A 'Yes, that was distracting, but luckily no harm done. I think someone was loading a difficult horse outside the school at the time.'

C 'So have I passed?'

A 'I'm afraid not quite today, you showed some good skills, you have a pleasant voice and got involved, but there were some problems too. I know the riders weren't very good, but even so you didn't really get to grips and give the riders enough help to develop the better way of going with their horses.'

C 'How could I coach well? The riders were much worse than I'm used to.'

A 'We had some problems getting riders for the assessment today and some riders who were booked to come cancelled, and that's why we used some less competent riders. It's a shame there was the drama with the loading as well. Even so I'm sorry that I can't pass you today. I'll fill out the form to itemise the key points.'

In summary, the two debriefs were similar but in the first the assessor *only* mentioned the weak areas, clearly and concisely so that there was only one avenue that Christopher had to accept and reflect on. In the first debrief the candidate was told very clearly that he had not been successful. His inadequacy to deliver to the standard required was clearly indicated. In the second debrief, the assessor gave two avenues that could have contributed to Christopher's weakness (the insecure, weak riders and the fraças in the car park). This could easily deflect Christopher into blaming the weak riders or the upset, as to being the reasons for his failure. His performance was not up to standard, but one assessor allowed Christopher to consider other causes of his failure, other than just his incompetence.

In delivering feedback, always invite self-feedback first from the recipient. If the individual is not forthcoming, then focus on their behaviour and invite an opinion on what might have been done differently. Keep your voice and body language very neutral and 'pull' (invite) first before 'pushing' (giving your advice).

In delivering feedback, give absolutely clear facts about what happened. Invite the recipient to then reflect on those facts and encourage or lead them into discussion about how an activity might be done in the future to generate a different or better outcome.

INSIGHTS

- The intangible aspects of agreeing a working contract are often overlooked.

- A good coach will develop an awareness of when information is not being 'absorbed' by the learner and be able to facilitate the learning in a different way.

- Communication is one of the keys to excellent coaching because unless we can communicate our knowledge, skill and competence to another person then those attributes stay locked inside us and therefore cannot benefit the learner.

- The coach should initiate a discussion which results in an agreed working contract. Ignore this important step at your peril.

- A great coach needs a wide repertoire of potential interventions, and the ability to assess the situation accurately so that they can employ the most appropriate behaviour, at the right time, with the correct degree of intensity.

- Good-quality feedback will add value to the learning process.Sometimes giving feedback will be difficult, so support and encouragement will be necessary to diffuse disappointment.

7. WHERE NEXT?

POINT OF VIEW

We hope that, regardless of your level of experience as a coach, you have read some or all of this publication to date, and feel encouraged to go on ... Where do we go from here? What more can we learn? The answers have to be: we can learn as much or as little as we choose, 'the sky really is the limit or beyond, to the end of that rainbow'.

We authors share a passion for what we do and we hope that has shone through in this book. We have enjoyed our writing collaboration and sharing our experience, and our desire is that you have gained some knowledge from our points of views, scenarios and insights.

So, much of this book has been about the development of the coach and learner. We have made reference to constantly moving forward and learning, regeneration and striving for further excellence. At the heart of all we do is the horse, and his welfare should always be at the forefront of how we work with him. As mentioned earlier, some years ago the FEI adopted the motto of the horse as 'the happy athlete'. This motto is fundamental to any activity involving the horse. This applies equally to the family horse kept at home, to horses capable of winning The Derby or The Grand National, to the equine athletes involved in all the equestrian disciplines that utilise the horse in some shared competitive activity. The welfare of this willing partner, so necessarily involved in our commitment to our vision and aims, but not able to take any leading part in directing them,

must be our primary consideration. This is especially so now that modern developments in sport, science, psychology, equipment, technical and logistical support have all contributed to and fuelled our commitment to greater success at every level.

LEGACY

The majority of equestrian coaches work frequently with riders of novice or medium competence within their riding ability. Some of these riders may then develop into the élite riders/competitors of the future. In any sphere of sport, it is the broad base of the pyramid from which the strength and future development of the discipline develops. Olympic riders learnt to ride somewhere: they were not born Olympians. They may have been born with the 'potential' for élite competence, but that ability had to be initiated, recognised, nurtured, developed, directed and produced. All of the Olympic disciplines (dressage/eventing/showjumping, para dressage), and the other disciplines that are involved in World Equestrian Games (vaulting, endurance, driving) have structures in place to identify and develop young talent. In all equestrianism there is an ongoing emphasis on the legacy that our development establishes for the future of our sport. So how does that legacy manifest itself? Icons of the sport leave their mark on development and training, of both horses and of riders. As we have referred to earlier in this book (see page 90) role models in sport leave a 'legacy'. The desire to emulate or copy best practice is always an endorsement of recognition of quality, especially if that quality produces success. In the three Olympic disciplines we have icons of the sport whom many young equestrians will aim to copy.

In eventing, Great Britain has produced figures such as Pippa Funnell (one of only two riders to have won the Grand Slam of eventing – Badminton, Burghley and Kentucky 4* events in the same twelve months), Zara Tindall (née Phillips), holder of World and European titles in the same year, Lucinda Green, six times winner of Badminton on six different horses, and William Fox-Pitt, prolific winner of 4* events and World/European and Olympic medals. New Zealand has produced eventing champions in the form of Sir Mark Todd and compatriots Blyth Tait and Andrew Nicholson. Germany has come to the fore in eventing, with Ingrid Klimke, Michael Jung, Frank Ostholt and Dirk Schrade proving they are multiple winners.

In showjumping, the Whitaker dynasty in Britain has produced prolific winners and producers of world-class horses (and riders) over four decades, while Germany has, for many years, consistently produced world-class and Olympic riders. The breeding of horses and development of riders in mainland European countries such as Germany, Holland and France has ensured a source of education for aspiring showjumping and dressage riders.

Probably the most iconic figure in British dressage, establishing a visible legacy within his ongoing competitive and coaching life, is Carl Hester MBE, FBHS. In association with Carl we consider the phenomenal success achieved by Charlotte Dujardin with the amazing horse Valegro. Carl's influence is clearly visible through the consistent success of an increasing number of talented riders and coaches who have served apprenticeships with Carl, and who are now consolidating that system of training and permeating it throughout their own riding and coaching.

All the élite riders mentioned, and many other worthy compatriots, provide an image of the 'role model' for equestrian sport and create a desire in aspiring riders and coaches to follow their methodology to success.

The horse is the overall winner in all this, as there is an increasing awareness that, to achieve the highest level of success in any discipline, it is the *quality* of the training that is important, rather than the frequency and intensity of the training. The horse benefits from the relationship to his natural way of life, and the attention to detail in terms of his physical well-being is applied to his advantage. The methods of assessing the fitness of both horse and rider are greatly enhanced through modern techniques of measuring and quantifying, and the veterinary and farriery management of the horse is better than ever.

The future of equestrian sport looks bright. As we strive to improve and develop further, with the welfare of the horse paramount, we can utilise knowledge and experience from other sports and from the business world. We must leave no stone unturned in our quest to be better today than yesterday. However, it should be understood that there is a difference between ambition and effort. There can be clear vision of the 'goal', there can be innate ambition to achieve that goal, but without effort and a structure for that effort, the goal, if achieved, is reached by luck rather than by planning. Lasting legacy requires vision, passion, structure and planning. Legacy requires icons of the sport to motivate young enthusiasm, and then planning and organisation from a strong governing body to implement a process that is identifiable and that anyone feels they can become involved in.

MENTORING WITHIN SPORT COACHING

Over the years, the term 'mentor' has gradually become associated with the idea of an older and/or more experienced person acting as a guide to a younger and/or less experienced person. Often a person will seek out mentoring at a time when they are facing an important life decision, such as a career choice. A mentor can help them think through the decision itself, make sure that the decision-making process is sound, and support them through the transition once a decision has been made.

Mentoring is increasingly recognised in sport as being a useful tool for passing on and sharing knowledge and skill from a more experienced coach to a developing coach. Mentoring can cover a range of relationships and be carried out in a wide variety of sporting environments. A structure may exist for a more formal agreement between mentor-coach and coach, or the arrangement can be more casual and be developed to suit the requirements of the two individuals involved. It is important to recognise the value of the mentoring process and the benefits that can be gained from it.

Those of you who would describe yourselves as 'career coaches' or 'professional coaches' may aspire to become a mentor to others. Often the motivation is to 'give something back …' Mentors are sometimes viewed as super-coaches who, in their wisdom, take a wider, deeper, longer-term view of the learner's developmental needs. (The word 'mentor' originally comes from Greek mythology – Ulysses entrusted the education of his son Telemachus to his old and faithful friend, Mentor.)

The roles of mentor and learner

A mentor may be defined as a coach who can share their own experience with others to promote thought, ideas and creativity. Through informal learning and a two-way process between mentor and learner, education takes place.

As a coach/learner, to have someone to whom you can turn for advice on any issue, in complete confidence, is of great value and support. There may be different individuals to whom you can turn, depending on the nature of the issue. A mentor is almost always another coach or someone involved on a parallel learning path, who can identify with the subject of concern and share experiences, in order to offer help or suggest solutions. A mentor can talk through the subject, promoting thought by offering new ideas on how or what to do. This two-way relationship can generate creativity. It can be powerful in challenging thinking and promoting more in-depth opinions on a subject. It provides an informal learning environment, where two colleagues can share new ideas in a two-way supportive environment. The mentor can become an informal facilitator who can act as an additional source of support, but who is not directly involved in the relationship between the coach and their learner. In this situation it is easier for both mentor and learner to discuss issues in a more detached and impartial way.

Consider the two scenarios below.

▶ EQUESTRIAN SCENARIO 1

Sam is anxious to improve as a coach and approaches an icon of the sport to see if he can come and watch her training her horses. The rider/coach Sam approached has Olympic, European and World Championship experience on British teams and has trained all her own horses, many of which were also home-bred. An arrangement is made between Sam and the rider, who is very happy for Sam to come to her yard and tells him she will be on her first horse at 6.30 a.m. Sam lives a couple of hours' drive away but takes the comment about the start time as being an indication of what time he should arrive (if he is as keen as he says he is!). Sam walks into the arena at 6.30 a.m. to find the rider already working her current international horse (she will be attending the European Championships in a few weeks' time). She greets Sam cheerily and says 'Great, you're just in time to look at my pirouettes!' Sam recoils at the suggestion that he could even begin to comment on, let alone contribute to an opinion of the quality of the pirouettes of this iconic rider! 'Come on' he is encouraged, 'just watch the hind legs coming into the movement and tell me if he is straight and how much weight you think he is taking back on his quarters within the movement.' Sam takes a deep breath and moves up to the arena boards and starts watching intently. Encouraged by the rider, a useful discussion develops between Sam and the rider as to what she is feeling in unison with what Sam is observing. Sam develops in confidence and is drawn into the observation and feedback on the pirouettes on both reins.

▶ EQUESTRIAN SCENARIO 2

Jan is a young coach working for her UKCC Level 2 qualification. She is confident and sure of herself, which can be useful attributes, but because she often feels she is right when others are wrong, she sometimes irritates those around her (both peer group and educators). At one coach training day Jan enters into a disagreement with her coach-educator, insisting that 'she is right' and implying that her coach-educator is misinformed. The coach-educator waits until Jan is on her own and then quietly says ' When you are an inexperienced coach it is generally quite useful to listen to other people's opinions, especially those with more experience than you. When you have some experience under your belt, then it can be useful to share your own opinions, which you will have gained through your own experience, but still listen to others and agree to differ if you feel your opinion is the one that is nearest to your beliefs and values. When you are an experienced coach, with years of practice in the industry, then it may be your right to be opinionated, especially if your experience can support that opinion. From my experience however, by the time you get to be the age when you can be opinionated, you can then learn so much more by just listening to everyone else and standing by what you know works for you.'

What can be learnt from these two scenarios?

- Wisdom! It cannot be learnt – it is acquired.

- The generosity of the top rider/coach to show that 'eyes on the ground', however inexperienced they might feel, could add another dimension of learning to that rider on that occasion.

- The encouragement felt by Sam, that someone of the calibre of this rider could value his opinion. Encouragement is awesome in its power to a learner. On this occasion it may well have changed the course of Sam's day – possibly his week and maybe even his life.

- The more experience you develop the more you can learn by watching and listening, not necessarily having to contribute an opinion of your own.

- Jan learning that, although she might 'know she was right', it is not always necessary or helpful to assert that opinion. Especially in a group situation, it can be valuable to learn from each other's opinions and take time to listen to different points of view, which may in turn broaden your own opinions.

Developing the mentor relationship

If we accept that mentoring is a powerful tool in the education and development of coaches at any level, then mentoring is about helping others create, recognise and expand their learning experiences. The authors would be able to identify several individuals who have been, and are still, influential in supporting and having an input on their self-awareness and personal development. A mentor may move into your life for a short or specific period and have a profound influence on that time of development (e.g. at school, university or during an apprenticeship). In other circumstances, a special and valued individual may stay in your life and even posthumously continue to 'whisper in your ear', to support and contribute to your thoughts, reflections and decisions in your work and life.

You may be *looking* for a mentor but, more often than not, the individual who moves into that role is a person who 'just happens to be in the right place at the right time' and the relationship has already commenced before you jointly recognise it as a mentoring opportunity.

Mentoring can and should be a satisfying role for both the mentor and learner. If both participants enter the relationship on equally contributing terms, then the benefits can be mutual. Let's consider what opportunities there are in a mentoring process, if it is identified as a one-to-one relationship to support the learner's development. The learner may be in any walk of life, although in our context we are thinking in terms of rider/coach/judge/businessperson/organiser. The opportunities might be:

- To create, expand and maximise learning experiences.

- To empower the learner to manage learning better for themselves by developing self-awareness and self-reflection.

- To establish an adaptable two-way relationship to support the specific needs of the learner, but also to ensure a fulfilling relationship for the mentor.

- Because of the practical nature of equestrian sport, mentoring can and should be a valuable, ongoing tool to help coaches to improve those practical skills.

A good mentor will be open-minded, up-to-date and forward-thinking. A good mentor will want others to succeed, will be confident in their own values, beliefs and competence and not reluctant to share these with others of similar or less experience. They will also have excellent listening skills, value other people's opinions and encourage initiative from their learner. They will lead by example and always set an example worthy of imitation, and encourage the learner to think by questioning, discussion and providing constructive feedback and guidance with consistency and honesty.

If we return to the philosophy that 'we never stop learning', which has been expressed several times in this book, why would anyone who is serious about 'wanting to be better' not have a mentor? A mentor is a always an asset. A friend, confidant(e), trusted individual, that wonderful 'sounding block' who may help you at a critical time, when you need to share a problem and gain either support or a different opinion before making a decision.

Look back at your life to date and identify those people who have fulfilled that role. As you proceed through your career, stay aware of individuals who could move into a mentoring role in due course. The equestrian industry is quite small and you are likely to meet many like-minded people in your progression. 'Networking' is essential; we should all be wanting to help each other for the good of the industry and ultimately for the welfare of the horse, who is a fundamental and essential part of our lives.

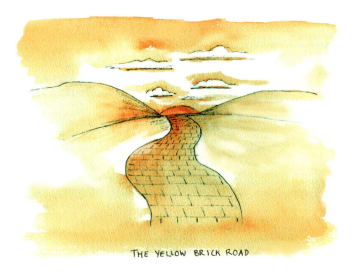

THE YELLOW BRICK ROAD

FURTHER DEVELOPMENT AS A COACH

In the previous chapters we have outlined the basic requirements and competencies for an effective coach. For those of you who want to excel and release surprising potential in yourselves and others, the following topics, such as meditation, may be of interest.

We spend the early part of our lives at school 'being educated' in the tried and tested subjects of 'reading, writing and arithmetic', plus an increasing range of subjects to suit every interest and desire for knowledge. Those of us who choose an equestrian career enter a world of 'vocational occupation'. An intrinsic passion drives us to follow this equestrian sport. Initially, most learners enter the activity through a fundamental desire to ride and be involved with the horse. Much further along the road, some riders develop a need or a desire to transfer the knowledge they have gained to other learners who are seeking to develop their riding skill. This book has covered many of the challenges that are met by both coach and learner, when forming a relationship that enables the knowledge of the coach to be transferred efficiently to the learner. The more talented and successful the coach has been as a rider, often the more difficult it is for them to be able to transfer that ability and technical skill successfully to another (perhaps less innately talented) rider. The transition from being a skilled rider to becoming an equally skilled coach takes time, commitment, patience and passion.

It is a recognised and accepted fact that attendance at coach education courses will increase the basic knowledge of a coach. Knowledge and understanding of 'how learning is achieved' and different methods of delivery will all be demonstrated and discussed. Coaching, however, requires a practical application and, in order to improve the effectiveness of the coach, observation, reflection and discussion are imperative.

Coaches at every level of experience should display a commitment to continually improving their effectiveness. This does not only require staying up to date with competition requirements, trends in management and training of horses, sport rules and regulations, but a commitment to remaining innovative, curious and inventive in striving for personal improvement.

For those of you who would like to delve further into the psychological aspects of coaching, understanding more about mindfulness may be of interest. Mindfulness includes a range of practices, such as meditation, that one can incorporate into daily life to break the cycle of anxiety. A recent study, led by Daniel Cherkin Ph.D. and published in the *Journal of the American Medical Association* (22 March 2016), also suggests that meditation eases chronic lower back pain. Given that this is an affliction that some riders have to deal with, whether it is a direct result of an equestrian-related incident, the impact of a general accident, or tension arising from stress, this could negatively impair the rider's effectiveness.

In addition to the topic being covered in some of the books listed in Further Reading, mindfulness workshops are available at the following personal growth centres:

- Mindfulness Stress Based Reduction (Bangor, Wales)

- Oxford University, Professor Mark Williams

- The Positive Mental Foundation, Edinburgh

- Centre for Mindfulness in Medicine, Healthcare and Society (USA)

- Institute for Mindfulness-Based Approaches (Germany)

- The Asian Leadership Institute (Asia)

- A CD on relaxation is available from: Zana@transformance.co.uk

- For more information on emotional resilience, please contact Professor David Peters at Westminster University's Centre for Resilience, London

Continuous professional development (CPD) is the expectation of every profession in the twenty-first century. Certification or a qualification validates the candidate's competence at the level achieved on that day, but does not guarantee maintenance of standards or improvement of competence through good training and experience, unless CPD is a commitment.

In equestrian sport there are countless opportunities to improve and develop through further training and experience. Many academic institutions run a range of courses from foundation degree to doctorate level, covering equestrian-related subjects. However, most coaches who are working 'in the field' will prefer to gain further skills in a practical environment. The three Olympic disciplines (showjumping, dressage and eventing) all run annual development days or 'forums' where a range of presenters will deliver a variety of subjects of practical interest and application to coaches of all levels. For example, for a number of years, the Global Dressage Forum has run annually in October. This coming together of the top riders, trainers and judges in this discipline, from all over the world, was initiated by the Bartel Family from Academy Bartels in Holland. It is an opportunity for discussion and observation of practical and theoretical subjects relating to the training of the horse, with an emphasis on dressage, but of relevance to all equestrian training and welfare. Days such as the International Event Forum held at Hartpury College, Gloucestershire, annually in the early part of the year, demonstrate subjects relevant to the training of the event horse and rider. Every equestrian discipline will advertise training and development through their own respective websites and national equestrian press.

In addition to attending such gatherings, some of the most valuable experience can be gained by watching a more experienced coach or rider at work. Most coaches are generous with their support of those wishing to gain more knowledge and experience by watching. Sitting in or writing for a dressage judge is another useful source of education. Writing for a vet at an endurance competition can give great insight into the fitness and training of horses in that discipline, and being a fence judge at an event, or helping to steward at any well-run competition, will give plenty of opportunity to see how riders manage stress and deal with disappointment, or the unexpected. Almost without exception, every equestrian situation will offer some opportunity to gain knowledge and therefore learning. The more open-minded and versatile you are, the more likely you are to seize every chance to learn.

We congratulate you and thank you for getting to this last page! We hope you have gained some knowledge and inspiration from reading this book – either the parts that interested you, or in its entirety. We hope it motivates you to continue your personal quest to develop as a coach, rider or both, and to enjoy your partner, the horse. We are so privileged and fortunate to enjoy the fascinating challenges, fun, endeavours and joys that these wonderful creatures share with us.

APPENDIX 1: Guidance for Establishing a Coaching Philosophy

- Your philosophy shapes the unique way in which YOU coach.
- Your philosophy will have a direct impact on the way you coach.
- Your values and beliefs are the set of principles that guide your practice as a coach – why you coach as you do.
- It provides boundaries within which the coach-learner relationship is formed.
- It should reflect your true beliefs and values (not what is politically correct or ideological).
- Regularly re-examine and re-evaluate your philosophy as your experiences shape and evolve your thoughts.
- As a coach you are in a position of authority and, as such, your opinions will often be taken as fact by others: 'My coach says …'
- If you have a set of principles then this will help you to manage dilemmas that arise, which challenge your philosophy versus practice (e.g. although in principle you expect 'total honesty', there might be a time to 'soften' the message to a rider over issues of selection or opinion on performance).
- Values are those social, moral and ethical standards that have been acquired over a lifetime and which underlie every decision and course of action.
- Understanding your values and how they influence your coaching philosophy is an important step for any coach.
- How do you incorporate your values into your day-to-day behaviour?
- How do your values as a coach shape the behaviour of your riders?
- How do you cope with the external pressures that conflict with your values (e.g. riders' expectations, pressures of achieving results, influence or pressure from 'significant others')?

You will need to find a compromise between your coaching philosophy and your practice.

Questions to help develop a coaching philosophy

The following questions may help you to develop your coaching philosophy:
- What is coaching and why do I think that?
- Why am I a coach?

- Have my motives for being a coach changed? How? Why?
- Who holds the power in the coach- or rider-led relationship?
- Are they 'my riders' or am I 'their coach'.
- What is my role as a coach and why do I think that?
- Why are these riders participating?
- Whose expectations am I fulfilling? Why?
- Why did a particular coach have such a meaningful impact on me?
- What are my future hopes, for the riders I coach and for myself as a coach?
- Is there a case for me to expand and explore the boundaries of the traditional coaching role?
- Do I want to do that and what are the implications of doing so?
- How can I allow my own personality to emerge through the coaching role?

What makes up a coaching philosophy?

- Think of a coach you respect. What qualities do they have that you admire?
- What are your core values?
- What principles make you the person you are?
- What are your beliefs as a coach?
- Prioritise your top three values and top three beliefs.
- Have these changed through your professional life as a coach to date?
- If so, what has changed them and why?

For example, do you believe:
- The rider needs as much information as possible?
- That you have to have 'done it' to be able to 'teach it'?
- That the rider performs better if you are there?
- That you should empower the rider to give their best performance without you being there?

What do YOU believe?

As a coach, do you:

- Shout.
- Listen.
- Ask questions.
- Not hear what your rider has to say.
- Not listen to the rider.
- Know best.
- Involve the rider.
- Never give up until you think it is right.

Are you:

- Always right.
- A hard task master.
- Focused.
- Caring.
- Thoughtful.
- Supportive.
- Knowledgeable.
- Stressed.
- Understanding.
- Aloof.
- Personable.
- Distant.
- Steady.
- Consistent.
- Moody.
- Reliable.
- Kind.
- Fair.
- Motivating.
- Funny.
- Helpful.
- Sympathetic.

(The list is really endless and contains good and not so good character traits!)

Some commonly held values

- Independence.
- Honesty.
- Integrity.
- Quality.
- Achievement.
- Happiness.
- Fame.
- Recognition.
- Stability.
- Friendship.
- Balance.
- Health.
- High earnings.
- Physical challenge.
- Pressure.
- Outdoor lifestyle.
- Security.
- Adventure.
- Personal development.
- Participation.
- Excitement.
- Power and authority.
- Change and variety.
- Status.
- Helping others.
- Fast pace.
- Time freedom.
- Flexibility.
- Challenging problems.
- Order.
- Work with others.
- Work with horses.

There are many others.

Establishing your philosophy as a coach will give you a foundation on which to project yourself. Think about it!

APPENDIX 2: British Equestrian Federation (BEF) Coaches' Code of Conduct

The BEF Coaches' Code of Conduct and Ethics, which is reproduced here by kind permission of the BEF, is built on the principles of integrity, fair play, equality, respect for others (including animals) and a sense of what is right. These ethical principles are integral, not optional, and apply to all levels of ability and commitment, including recreational equestrian activity as well as competitive equestrian sport. This code is a guide for good practice and it is required of all Member Bodies of the BEF accredited coaches that they will abide by these principles.

Coaches have a responsibility to support and promote their equestrian discipline and its governing body, maintain standards of appearance and conduct and act with due respect for the reputation of the governing body.

Safety

Coaches share with riders the responsibility for rider and horse safety. Coaches are also responsible for ensuring, as far as is reasonably possible, the creation and maintenance of a safe environment for helpers and bystanders.

Coaches must ensure they keep abreast of approved coaching practice determined by their member body and other relevant organisations.

All training should take account of the age, maturity, experience and ability of both rider and horse.

Coaches have a duty to protect riders from harm and abuse and in particular should understand the duty of care when working with young (U18) and vulnerable people. Coaches should consult the BEF *Safeguarding Children and Vulnerable Adults* policy for additional guidance and information.

All coaches will be required to attend a Safeguarding Children workshop prior to certification.

Coaches must ensure that adequate insurance cover for all aspects of their coaching and training is in place.

Coaches and those in support must place the well-being and safety of both horse and rider above the development of performance.

Coaches should work with other specialists as necessary, for example, officials, vets and other coaches.

Competence

It is expected that equestrian coaches will hold up-to-date nationally recognised governing body teaching/coaching qualifications and/or other relevant accreditation.

Coaches must confine themselves to practise in those areas for which their training and competence are recognised by their Member Body of the BEF.

Coaches have a responsibility to themselves and their participants to maintain their effectiveness as an equestrian coach and should regularly seek ways to develop their personal and professional development, taking advantages of opportunities provided.

Coaches should plan and prepare for sessions. Their participants should have a programme that is appropriate and progressive.

Personal standards

Coaches should display high personal standards and project a favourable image of equine activity to Member Bodies of the BEF, performers, parents and the wider public.

Appropriate dress codes should be followed whilst training and competing as laid down by the Member Body.

Coaches must be a positive role model and behave appropriately at all times.

Confidentiality

Coaches are in a position where they gather personal information about riders in the course of a working relationship. The disclosure and use of information gathered is the subject of the Data Protection Act. Coaches must ensure that agreement is reached with riders/participants or their parents/guardians about the collection, storage and potential boundaries of sharing information.

Integrity

Coaches must not compromise any rider by advocating measures which could constitute unfair advantage or that may jeopardise the safety or well-being of rider or horse. In the event of a registered coach being convicted of an offence involving cruelty to animals, the Member Body may, at its sole discretion, rescind the registered status of that coach and may subject the coach to disciplinary proceedings.

Coaches must not maliciously or recklessly injure or attempt to injure, whether directly or indirectly, the professional reputation, prospects or business of their Member Body of the BEF or any other Member Body or coach.

Coaches should prepare riders to respond to success and failure in a dignified manner and treat opponents with respect.

Coaches have a responsibility to instil good values and behaviour in their riders and discourage inappropriate behaviour in training and competition.

Coaches must not act in any way, nor publish any matter, such that the action or publication may be interpreted as carrying the authority of the Member Body of the BEF unless they have specific authority from the Member Body to do so.

Coaches should operate in an open environment with transparent communication and actions. Where possible coaches should share their knowledge and experience.

Coaches must at all times observe the rules and regulations made from time to time by the Member Bodies of the BEF as they apply to coaches.

Humanity

Coaches must treat all riders equitably and respect the rights and dignity of all individuals with whom they work.

Coaches and those in support must place the well-being and safety of both horse and rider above the development of performance.

Coaches should always promote the positive aspects of our sport (e.g. fair play) and must never condone rule violations or the use of prohibited substances.

Coaches must ensure that all employees in any equestrian business or establishment under their control comply with the standards laid down from time to time by Member Bodies of the BEF and follow all appropriate legal and ethical considerations to ensure open and fair recruitment processes and working conditions. Please see BEF Equity Policy for additional guidance and information.

Any failure on the part of a coach to comply with the provisions of this code may render the coach liable to disciplinary proceedings by their Member Body.

Safeguarding children and vulnerable adults

Newly qualifying coaches at UKCC Level 2 and above are required to undergo an enhanced disclosure via the Disclosure and Barring Service in order to register or become affiliated to coach within the BEF or by a Member Body. Existing qualified coaches will be required to undergo an enhanced disclosure via the Disclosure Barring Service to retain current coaches' registration/affiliation within the BEF or by a Member Body. Coaches may be asked to produce their certificate as required.

In the event of a registered coach being convicted of an offence that is relevant to their role, the Member Body may at its sole discretion rescind the registered status of that coach and may subject the coach to disciplinary proceedings.

Coaches should ensure that physical contact is appropriate, carried out using the necessary guidelines and consent and approval is given where possible.

Coaches must receive, record and report allegations of abuse according to BEF guidelines.

Coaches should avoid any form of sexual contact or inappropriate behaviour with any participants but specifically those who are under age or vulnerable.

Any abuse of trust (sexual activity or relationships where an adult holds a position of authority, influence or responsibility over a participant) may result in disciplinary action by the BEF Member Body or organisation.

Coaches should communicate with participants in an appropriate recognised format and should be aware that social networking sites are a very popular medium of communication with many aged much younger than 18 years. Many centres/schools will now host their own social networking sites or pages. One to one interaction via email, text messages or social networks particularly with those under 18 should be avoided. Further guidance is available from the BEF, your BEF Member Body and the Child Protection in Sport Unit.

Equity and equal opportunities

With regard to equity, the British Equestrian Federation:

- aims to ensure that all people, irrespective of race, gender, ability, ethnic origin, social status or sexual orientation, have equal opportunities to take part in equestrianism at all levels and roles;
- seeks to educate and guide BEF members, their employees and volunteers on the ownership, adoption and implementation of its Equity Plan;
- intends to raise awareness of Equity through the implementation of this policy and the adoption of the Equity Plan; and, as a result of this process;
- aims to monitor, review and evaluate progress in achieving the stated aims and objectives and to feed back to member organisations on progress made.

BEF will ensure that its recruitment and selection procedures are fair and transparent, and meet the appropriate legal requirements. Each Member Body will ensure its own procedures meet these requirements.

FURTHER READING

Auty, Islay, *Progressive School Exercises for Dressage and Jumping*, Kenilworth Press (2001) ISBN 1-872119-38-7

Auty, Islay, *Coaching Skills for Riding Teachers*, Kenilworth Press (2008) ISBN 978-1-905693-08-5

Bandler, Richard & Grinder, John *The Structure of Magic*, Science and Behaviour Books (1975) ISBN 08314-0044-7

Bandler, Richard & Grinder, John, *The Structure of Magic II*, Science and Behaviour Books (1976) ISBN 08314-0049-8

Borgoyne and Reynolds, *Management Learning Integrating Perspectives in Theory and Practice*, Sage (2000) ISBN 0-8039-7644-5

Goleman, Daniel, *Emotional Intelligence*, Bloomsbury Publishing Plc (1996) ISBN 0-7475-2830-6

Goleman, Daniel, *Working with Emotional Intelligence*, Bloomsbury (1999) ISBN 0-7475-4384-4

Hansen, Dr Sven, *Inside-Out: The Practice of Resilience*, Sven Hansen (2015) ISBN 978-0-473-30689-2

Hawkins, Peter, and Smith, Nick, *Coaching, Mentoring and Organizational Consultancy (Supervision and Development)* Oxford University Press (2007) ISBN 0-335-21815-6

Heaversedge, Dr Jonty & Halliwell, Ed, *The Mindful Manifest*, Hay House UK (2012) ISBN 978-1-84850-824-8

Heron, John, *Helping the Client*, Sage (1990) ISBN 0-8039-8291-7

Humphrey, Keith, *Regeneration & Co-Creation: Changing Change*, Core Context Consulting Ltd (2008) ISBN 978-0-9558449-0-4

Jeffers, Susan, *Feel The Fear and Do It Anyway*, Vermilion (2007) ISBN 978-0-091907-07-5

Maister, David, Green, Charles and Galford, Robert, *The Trusted Advisor*, Simon & Schuster UK (2002) ISBN 0-7432-0776-9

O'Neill, Mary Beth, *Executive Coaching with Backbone and Heart*, Jossey-Bass (2000) ISBN 0-7879-5016-5

Williams, Mark and Penman, Danny, *Mindfulness: A practical guide to finding peace in a frantic world*, Piatkus (2011) ISBN 978-0-7499-5308-9

Yanhelovich, Daniel, *The Magic of Dialogue*, Simon & Schuster (2001) ISBN 1-85788-256-3

USEFUL CONTACT DETAILS

Amongst its other aims and objectives, the British Horse Society administers a progressive structure of development and examinations for those intending to make a career in coaching riders. British Dressage, British Eventing and British Showjumping are the UK organisations representing the Olympic equestrian disciplines.

The British Horse Society, Abbey Park, Stareton, Kenilworth,
Warwickshire, CV8 2XZ
Tel: 02476 840500 Website: www.bhs.org.uk

British Dressage, Meriden Business Park, Copse Drive, Meriden,
West Midlands, CV5 9RG.
Tel: 02476 698830 Website: www.britishdressage.co.uk

British Eventing, Abbey Park, Stareton, Kenilworth,
Warwickshire CV8 2RN
Tel: 02476 69 8856 Website: www.britisheventing.com

The British Showjumping Association, Meriden Business Park, Copse Drive, Meriden,
West Midlands, CV5 9RG
Tel: 02476 698800 Website: www.britishshowjumping.co.uk

INDEX